UNDERSTANDING THE WORLD IN LIGHT OF BIBLE PROPHECY

ALSO FROM REVIVAL TODAY

Financial Overflow

Dominion Over Sickness and Disease

Boldly I Come: Praying According to God's Word

Twenty Secrets for an Unbreakable Marriage

How to Dominate in a Wicked Nation

Seven Wrong Relationships

Everything a Man Should Be

Understanding the World in Light of Bible Prophecy

Books are available in EBOOK and PAPERBACK through your favorite online book retailer or by request from your local bookstore.

UNDERSTANDING THE WORLD
IN LIGHT OF BIBLE PROPHECY

JONATHAN SHUTTLESWORTH

Foreword by
TIFF SHUTTLESWORTH

Unless otherwise indicated, all Scripture quotations are taken from the Holy Bible, New Living Translation, copyright © 1996, 2004, 2015 by Tyndale House Foundation. Used by permission of Tyndale House Publishers, a Division of Tyndale House Ministries, Carol Stream, Illinois 60188. All rights reserved.

Book design by eBook Prep:
www.ebookprep.com

January 2023
eBook ISBN: 978-1-64457-291-7
Paperback ISBN: 978-1-64457-292-4
Hardcover ISBN: 978-1-64457-591-8

Rise UP Publications
644 Shrewsbury Commons Ave, Ste 249
Shrewsbury PA 17361
United States of America
www.riseUPpublications.com
Phone: 866-846-5123

The goal of life is not to simply stay alive.

— JONATHAN SHUTTLESWORTH

FOREWORD

I will never forget the first words that I spoke to Jonathan, our first child and only son. I whispered in his ear, "you don't know it yet, but one day you are going to be a great man of God."

From his infancy, and throughout all the stages of his childhood development, Jonathan always had a special awareness of the things of God, and a growing hunger to learn and understand the Bible. At the age of six, he read the Bible every day, and from cover to cover, using a 'one-year' Bible reading plan. He immersed himself in the study of the scriptures.

Throughout his entire life, he heard my messages in our Lost Lamb Crusades on Bible Prophecy. As my son, he had a behind-the-scenes look at my passion for studying, understanding, and preaching on eschatology, and my desire to help people understand the fundamentals of Bible prophecy and end-time events.

For many Christians, and serious students of the Scriptures, Bible prophecy is an intimidating subject; sadly, many are afraid to approach it. I have always reminded my audiences that Bible prophecy is not to scare you but to prepare you.

How often the Scriptures reference a particular topic or subject helps us discern its significance and doctrinal weight. In the study of theology, this is called; "The Law of Proportion."

Did you know that 28.5% of the Old Testament is prophecy? And 21.5% of the New Testament is prophecy? 27% of the Bible is prophecy! It is impossible to be a serious student of the Bible and not be a serious student of Bible prophecy!

Prophecy is what separates the Bible from all other religious books. No other religious books contain prophetic content! The Bible is a book of prophecy—prophecy being fulfilled with complete and total accuracy. Bible prophecy is still relevant today. In fact, it is more up-to-date than tomorrow's headlines. One Bible prophecy scholar said, "Bible prophecy is so accurate it is history written before it takes place."

Did you know that God promised a special blessing to all who study Bible prophecy? The book of Revelation is the only book in the entirety of the Bible that begins with a supernatural promise of favor to its readers.

Revelation 1:3 God blesses the one who reads the words of this prophecy to the church, and he blesses all who listen to its message and obey what it says, for the time is near.

The book of Revelation is the only book in the Bible containing this blessing! I have often wondered if Almighty God, knowing the power and priority of Bible prophecy, gave this special blessing to motivate us not to ignore its message!

As you read this book, purpose in your heart to become a dedicated student of Bible prophecy. Perhaps the greatest benefit you will gain from a better understanding of Bible prophecy and end-time events is preparation to spiritually navigate these final hours of human history and live ready to meet the Lord!

Bible prophecy reminds us, there is an eternity, there is life after death, there is a heaven to gain, there is a hell to shun, and there is a day of judgment. May the truths you discover in this book keep the urgency of living for Christ ablaze in your spirit.

> Therefore be ye also ready: for in such an hour as ye
> think not the Son of man cometh.

> — MATTHEW 24:44 KJV

Reaching the unreached,
Evangelist Tiff Shuttlesworth

INTRODUCTION TO BIBLE PROPHECY

INTRODUCTION

There is a great need for understanding Bible prophecy in today's world. Anyone with a proper understanding of Bible prophecy would not have shut their church down for COVID. There's next-to-no understanding of what the Bible says concerning prophecy within modern churches. The problem is that prophecy is not preached. Considering the number of preachers that closed their churches, you can see the lack of understanding I am talking about.

There exists an active plan of the Devil to destroy planet Earth and destroy the Church. Unfortunately, many Christians can't spot it because every church service is just "Three Keys to a Better Life." But one of the largest parts of the Bible is prophecy. When studying Bible prophecy, there are two questions we must cover. First, are Bible prophecies reliable? Second, what are you personally willing to die for?

During the first 10 years of my ministry, I opened Sunday morning with the third chapter of Second Peter. I found the best way to wake up a dead church was for them to realize that Jesus is coming soon. Christians would be the most miserable people on the planet if Bible prophecy were not true because everything that they're doing would be for nothing. However, there is a resurrection, and when you understand it, it puts passion into your life.

What did Paul say about the resurrection?

> ...if there will be no resurrection from the dead?
> And if there is no resurrection, "Let's feast and
> drink, for tomorrow we die!"
>
> — 1 CORINTHIANS 15:32

It is easy to spot a preacher who does not believe in the soon return of Christ. Their preaching has something missing; there is no passion. There are no tears in the eyes; there is no onus to get the gospel out.

What can you do if you can't find a great Holy Ghost church in your area and can't move because of a job? Get another job and move! If you find yourself saying something like, "I have a job, so I can't move, but I don't have a good church," you've got it wrong. *The church is first.*

With the way people's priorities are, you would think the Bible says, "Seek ye second the kingdom of God, after you get a good job and a nice place to live in a good neighborhood, get your kids in a good school, get them a good education and then get them in cheering and soccer and wrestling. And then, with what time is leftover, see if you can find time for a good church."

> This is my second letter to you, dear friends, and in
> both of them I have tried to stimulate your
> wholesome thinking and refresh your memory. I
> want you to remember what the holy prophets
> said long ago and what our Lord and Savior
> commanded through your apostles.
> Most importantly, I want to remind you that in the
> last days scoffers will come, mocking the truth

and following their own desires. They will say,
"What happened to the promise that Jesus is
coming again? From before the times of our
ancestors, everything has remained the same
since the world was first created."

They deliberately forget that God made the heavens
long ago by the word of his command, and he
brought the earth out from the water and
surrounded it with water. Then he used the water
to destroy the ancient world with a mighty flood.
And by the same word, the present heavens and
earth have been stored up for fire. They are being
kept for the day of judgment, when ungodly
people will be destroyed.

But you must not forget this one thing, dear friends:
A day is like a thousand years to the Lord, and a
thousand years is like a day. The Lord isn't really
being slow about his promise, as some people
think. No, he is being patient for your sake. He
does not want anyone to be destroyed, but wants
everyone to repent.

— 2 PETER 3:1-9

Everything we do revolves around winning souls. According to 2 Peter 3:9, the only reason Christ hasn't returned is to give more time for people to be saved. Therefore, you can ascertain that the less your ministry and life revolve around soul-winning, the less blessed and the less anointed they will be. The more you commit to going into the harvest field and winning souls, plucking them out of darkness, and bringing them into light, the more blessed and anointed you will be. The farmer has long patience for the precious fruit of the earth. If you build your life to lay that precious fruit at the feet of Jesus, you enjoy health and blessing for free. Did Billy Graham ever pursue prosperity? No. If you had asked him, he probably would have said he was against it. And yet, he had the richest ministry in the United States. How could that be? Because God has one focus: the winning of the lost.

> But the day of the Lord will come as unexpectedly
> as a thief. Then the heavens will pass away with
> a terrible noise, and the very elements them-
> selves will disappear in fire, and the earth and
> everything on it will be found to deserve
> judgment.
>
> — 2 PETER 3:10

In my mind, this passage describes nuclear war. The Bible says God will never destroy the earth again with a flood, but it never says He won't destroy the earth again. The present earth is being stored up for fire. The heavens will pass away with a terrible noise, and the heat will melt the elements themselves. That requires intense heat, and the Bible says it will be in the sky.

> Since everything around us is going to be destroyed
> like this, what holy and godly lives you should
> live, looking forward to the day of God and
> hurrying it along. On that day, he will set the
> heavens on fire, and the elements will melt away
> in the flames. But we are looking forward to the
> new heavens and new earth he has promised, a
> world filled with God's righteousness.
> And so, dear friends, while you are waiting for these
> things to happen, make every effort to be found
> living peaceful lives that are pure and blameless
> in his sight.
> And remember, our Lord's patience gives people
> time to be saved.
>
> — 2 PETER 3:11-15

The Lord is waiting so people have time to be saved. I'll tell you a secret to life: it's not "God bless what I'd like to do;" instead, it's: "God, I have just found out what you want me to do. As your servant, I'll throw myself at the task of getting lost people saved with all my might." As you do, you get the resources of the one you're serving because you are doing His work.

Let's define some terms upfront. The next event on God's prophetic calendar is the Rapture of the Church of the Lord Jesus Christ. As soon as you say rapture, you'll have a contingent of Christians start talking about some guy in upstate New York as if that's where the doctrine of the Rapture started. They'll say the Rapture is nowhere in the Bible. The word "rapture" is not in the Bible because the Bible was not written in English. It was written in Greek, and the Greek word is *harpazo*, which was then translated into Latin, *raptures* or *rapturo*, where the word "rapture" comes from. The Rapture is the great catching away of the saints, during which Jesus' feet will never touch the ground, and we will meet Him in the air.

Following the Rapture of the Church of the Lord Jesus Christ is the seven-year Tribulation Period. This will be the worst time the world has ever known and will end with a war called Armageddon. During Armageddon, all the armies of Earth are gathered to make war against Israel. As they attack Israel, Christ returns with His Church. Remember that the Holy Spirit is never removed from the earth during each event.

The second coming is Christ returning with the Church, ushering in the millennium. I won't go into great depth about the millennium; I like dealing with Bible things that affect our present lives.

The first thing I need you to understand about Bible prophecy is that God is a God of times and seasons.

> From the tribe of Issachar, there were 200 leaders of
> the tribe with their relatives. All these men
> understood the signs of the times and knew the
> best course for Israel to take.
>
> — 1 CHRONICLES 12:32

15

> ...of the sons of Issachar who had understanding of
> the times, to know what Israel ought to do, their
> chiefs were two hundred; and all their brethren
> were at their command.
>
> — 1 CHRONICLES 12:32 (NKJV)

By knowing the times you are in, you can know what course the nation should take. For example, how can Rodney Howard-Browne, pastor of The River Church in Tampa, FL, get arrested for keeping his church open while other pastors say things like, "Right now we should be shepherds who care about the safety of our flock," while closing their churches and staying home until their Department of Health tells them it's okay to meet again? One understands Bible prophecy and can spot an antichrist spirit, while the other does not know God's times and seasons. Rodney Howard-Browne knew the best course to take by knowing times and seasons. Those who do not understand times and seasons don't know what path to take; their actions are dictated by heathens.

> It was the first year of the reign of Darius the Mede,
> the son of Ahasuerus, who became king of the
> Babylonians. During the first year of his reign, I,
> Daniel, learned from reading the word of the
> Lord, as revealed to Jeremiah the prophet, that
> Jerusalem must lie desolate for seventy years. So
> I turned to the Lord God and pleaded with him in
> prayer and fasting. I also wore rough burlap and
> sprinkled myself with ashes.
> I prayed to the Lord my God and confessed...
>
> — DANIEL 9:1-4

Daniel realized that Jerusalem had to be in exile for 70 years from reading Jeremiah's writings. However, the 70 years were up, and they were still exiled. Daniel understood from reading Jeremiah that the time of their captivity had ended prophetically but knew they were still captive. He started fasting and praying to break his people out because he understood God's prophetic timetable. Keep your eyes on God's calendar, not man's calendar. In doing so, like Daniel, you will live differently.

I'll tell you one of the greatest stories in the Bible. Enoch was a prophet who walked closely with God. Enoch had a son named Methuselah, who had a son named Lamech, who had a son named Noah. Which one of those names stands out as not being like the other? Enoch, two syllables. Lamech, two syllables. Noah, two syllables. Methuselah, four syllables. Enoch, as a prophet, named his son Methuselah, which is not a name but a sentence meaning, "when he comes to his end, then it shall come." Why was Noah so confident building the Ark? Because his great-grandfather named his son "when he dies, it will come." As Noah watched his grandfather getting older, he knew the time was coming. Some Bible scholars say that the flood came within seven days of when Methuselah died. The seven days essentially left Noah time to bury his grandfather, and then it came just like God spoke through Enoch.

IS BIBLE PROPHECY RELIABLE?

Do you know why many people never touch the book of Revelation, Paul's writings on Bible prophecy, or Matthew 24? Because they know that some Bible prophecy teachers said Mikhail Gorbachev would be the Antichrist. And when it turned out that he wasn't, those teachers lost credibility in their ministries. There are grey areas in Bible prophecy, like what the seven horns on the beast represent. Still, there are concrete, lock, stock, and barrel Bible prophecies that you don't have to read into.

> We will not all die, but we will all be transformed! It
> will happen in a moment, in the blink of an eye,
> when the last trumpet is blown. For when the
> trumpet sounds, those who have died will be
> raised to live forever. And we who are living will
> also be transformed.

> — 1 CORINTHIANS 15:51-52

> Then, together with them, we who are still alive and
> remain on the earth will be caught up in the
> clouds to meet the Lord in the air. Then we will
> be with the Lord forever.

> — 1 THESSALONIANS 4:17

These verses are not symbolic; this is literal speech. When interpreting the Bible, always take the Bible literally, and when it is not possible, search for the literal meaning. There are many parts of the Bible about prophecy that are literal. Christ will touch down on the Mount of Olives and split it in half. Specific nations will go to war against Israel. These are not figurative.

Is Bible prophecy reliable? Bible prophecy is not only reliable, but even critics of the Bible have referred to it as history written before it takes place.

It's a shame that many people avoid Bible prophecy because there's a book in the Bible called Revelation that says, *"Blessed is the one who reads aloud the words of this prophecy."* There is a blessing for digging into Bible prophecy. It's not surprising why the enemy wants to keep people out of it. Some people will say, "I don't get into that because whether Jesus comes pre-trib, mid-trib, or post-trib, I'm just going to be ready, whether He comes today or 1000 years from now." Would you talk about other doctrines like that? Would you say, "Whether there's healing or not, I'm just going to try to be my healthiest?" No, you dig into the Bible and seek out an understanding of healing.

In Isaiah 41:23, while mocking idols, God said, *"Tell us what the future holds, so we may know that you are gods."* The Devil doesn't know what will happen five minutes from now. He's not all-knowing; he is a created being. God knows the end from the beginning. He says, *"I am the Alpha and the Omega—the beginning and the end," says the Lord God. "I am the one who is, who always was, and who is still to come—the Almighty One."* This is what separates the Bible from the Quran and from the teachings of Buddha. They don't know what's happening, and they don't attempt to. The Devil does not know the future. If he did, do you think he would have crucified Christ? The Bible says, in 1 Corinthians 2:8, that had the rulers of this world known, they would not have crucified the Lord. Satan does not operate in God's realm of intelligence, but God gave us His intelligence through His Word, the Bible. God knows the future better than we know the past, and He has revealed it to us.

Perhaps the greatest and most obvious testimony to the accuracy of Biblical prophecy is provided by the people and nation of Israel. The Jews went without a homeland for 1900 years, just as God had promised numerous times in the Old Testament, as a reluctant judgment on His rebellious chosen people. In Deuteronomy 28:64, Moses warned Israel that if they corrupted themselves, the Lord would scatter them among all people from one end of the earth to the other. Remarkably, in 1948 God restored the Jews to their ancient homeland, fulfilling many other specific Old Testament prophecies. Throughout history, "the wandering Jew" has been hated and despised. Yet, despite unbelievable persecution, the Jews somehow managed to maintain their identity, such that when God's time-clock warranted, they were able to regroup as a nation in their ancient homeland.

When people move to another nation, their culture usually dies out in just two generations. My wife's parents are from Puerto Rico. My father-in-law speaks limited English. He recreated Puerto Rico in Boston; he would get in trouble for keeping chickens in his neighborhood. His daughter married me, a white guy, and she got Americanized. Now our daughter, Camila, speaks no Spanish. In two generations, it's gone, and that's how it goes everywhere. Yet, throughout 1900 years of persecution, the Jewish people still kept their clothing and culture. For 1900 years, they kept their language alive in all the world's nations and often married each other. That is a major testament to Bible prophecy.

In Matthew 24, Jesus said the fig tree will bud again. Did you know that people who studied the Bible before World War II tried to explain away those prophecies? They'd write, "Well, I know the Bible says that the fig tree will bud again, but there's obviously no way that can happen. That land is inhabited by the enemies of the Jewish people. How would they ever get Israel back?"

Then, to make it worse, Satan raised up Adolf Hitler with the satanic mission to wipe out the Jewish population. But, like everything he does, Satan's plans ultimately fail. The harsh persecution against the Jews put it in their hearts to seek their homeland, and another prophecy was fulfilled. Can a nation be born in a day? It was one day, on May 14th, 1948, that Israel was reborn. Here are the Jewish people with God's hand on them. God said, *"I will bless those that bless you. I will curse those that curse you."* It's a tough thing to bet your eternity against the Bible. Anyone can verify the numerous fulfilled prophecies of such cities as Sidon, Edom, Sumeria, and nations such as Egypt, Babylon, and Rome.

> They will destroy the walls of Tyre and tear down its
> towers. I will scrape away its soil and make it a
> bare rock! It will be just a rock in the sea, a place
> for fishermen to spread their nets, for I have
> spoken, says the Sovereign Lord. Tyre will
> become the prey of many nations...
>
> — EZEKIEL 26: 4-5

The Tyre prophecy is one of 1500 Old Testament prophecies about cities or nations that have already been fulfilled.

There will be no rulers left in Egypt...

— EZEKIEL 30:13

2,500 years have passed since this prophecy, and not one of the numerous ruling princes in Egypt has been Egyptian. This would be similar to me predicting there will be no more American presidents and it coming true.

Dr. D. James Kennedy wrote about an encounter with a Jewish man who said he did not believe in Christ. Dr. Kennedy responded that he was sorry to hear that, since Jesus is the Messiah of the Jewish people promised in their books. He then shared a few verses of scripture:

> Everyone who sees me mocks me. They sneer and shake their heads, saying, "Is this the one who relies on the Lord? Then let the Lord save him! If the Lord loves him so much, let the Lord rescue him!"

— PSALM 22:7-8

When that thief said that on the cross, he was fulfilling Psalm 22.

> But he was pierced for our rebellion, crushed for our sins. He was beaten so we could be whole. He was whipped so we could be healed.

— ISAIAH 53:5

Remember, these are Old Testament scriptures.

> Even my best friend, the one I trusted completely, the one who shared my food, has turned against me.

— PSALM 41:9

> My enemies surround me like a pack of dogs; an evil
> gang closes in on me. They have pierced my
> hands and feet.
>
> — PSALM 22:16

> Therefore I will give him a portion among the great,
> and he will divide the spoils with the strong,
> because he poured out his life unto death, and
> was numbered with the transgressors. For he
> bore the sin of many, and made intercession for
> the transgressors.
>
> — ISAIAH 53:12 (NIV)

> "And I will pour out on the house of David and the
> inhabitants of Jerusalem a spirit of grace and
> supplication. They will look on me, the one they
> have pierced, and they will mourn for him as one
> mourns for an only child, and grieve bitterly for
> him as one grieves for a firstborn son."
>
> — ZECHARIAH 12:10 (NIV)

When Dr. Kennedy finished reading these scriptures to the Jewish man, he asked him to whom these verses were referring. The man responded, "Obviously, they're talking about Jesus; so what?" Dr. Kennedy then pointed out that all the verses he had just read were from the Old Testament. The man was stunned and demanded to see the passages with his own eyes.

Did you know that crucifixion wasn't invented when David wrote Psalm 22? According to secular sources, crucifixion was invented as a method of capital punishment no earlier than the sixth century B.C. This is four centuries after

David wrote, *"they have pierced my hands and my feet."* The Old Testament contains 333 prophecies regarding the Messiah, most of which were fulfilled by the first coming of Christ. Mathematicians have shown that the odds of these prophecies being fulfilled in one man are greater than the number of atoms in the universe. Is Bible prophecy reliable? Yes. The rebirth of Israel began a countdown. When did the last days begin? On the day of Pentecost:

> Then Peter stepped forward with the eleven other apostles and shouted to the crowd, "Listen carefully, all of you, fellow Jews and residents of Jerusalem! Make no mistake about this. These people are not drunk, as some of you are assuming. Nine o'clock in the morning is much too early for that. No, what you see was predicted long ago by the prophet Joel:
> 'In the last days,' God says, 'I will pour out my Spirit upon all people. Your sons and daughters will prophesy. Your young men will see visions, and your old men will dream dreams.
> In those days I will pour out my Spirit even on my servants—men and women alike—and they will prophesy.
> And I will cause wonders in the heavens above and signs on the earth below—blood and fire and clouds of smoke.
> The sun will become dark, and the moon will turn blood red before that great and glorious day of the Lord arrives.
> But everyone who calls on the name of the Lord will be saved.'"
>
> — ACTS 2:14-21

Peter said in the Bible that the last days began on the day of Pentecost— almost 2000 years ago. So, we're not in the last days, but in the final moments of the last days.

WHAT ARE YOU PERSONALLY WILLING TO DIE FOR?

I am not afraid of anything in this world. I'm certainly not afraid of some damn flu, and I use that word biblically. I am not going to stop the work of the Lord for some bacteria or virus. I'm not going to be an idiot. I'm going to be courteous. I'm going to do my best to be gracious, but I am not going to stop building the church for some demonic virus or some demonic mandate. I am on a mission for the Lord Jesus Christ. Is that too honest, pastor? Jesus said, "I'll build my church." That's my mandate. I'm not playing games. Many of you that know my ministry know that nobody's going to stop me. If it means I have to go to prison, I'll go to prison. If it means they put me on a firing squad, I'll be on a firing squad, preaching to the last person loading their weapon. I am on a holy mission and holy men don't take orders from un-holy men.

— TIFF SHUTTLESWORTH

The LORD has given me a strong warning not to think like everyone else does. He said, "Don't call everything a conspiracy, like they do, and don't live in dread of what frightens them. Make the LORD of Heaven's Armies holy in your life. He is the one you should fear. He is the one

who should make you tremble. He will keep you
safe."

— ISAIAH 8: 11-14

In this last hour, you're going to have one of two spirits operating in you.
One of them is going to dictate your life.

> And we have received God's Spirit (not the world's
> spirit), so we can know the wonderful things
> God has freely given us.

— I CORINTHIANS 2:12

We're coming to the final moments, and the good news is that God doesn't
have us here just to get run over by the Antichrist. Rather, God has us here
as the restrainer against the forces of darkness. But if you lay down and
give up, what good are you?

Recently, Boko Haram terrorists attacked the Redeemed Christian Church
of God in Askira-Uba LGA of Borno state, Nigeria.[1] In the attack, a pastor
from Akure in Ondo state, Taiwo Dokun, was butchered by the terrorists.
Hear what a church member said about the attack that killed 25 people:

> "The pastor was in his house at about six in the morning when the
> insurgents attacked the village. His house was surrounded by hood-
> lums, and while attempting to run, he was shot. He was running to a
> neighbor's house, and it was in the course of his fleeing that he was
> shot in the head and chest, and then the insurgents came to butcher
> his body with swords. Then terrorists went into the pastor's house
> and burned it down and may have abducted the pastor's wife and
> three children who were inside the house of the attack."

Either they were burned alive in their home or captured by Islamic jihadists
and raped. Pastors in America get worried by mean Facebook comments.

Do you really expect churches that close for a half-inch of snow to fight government tyranny? If salt loses its flavor, how can you make it salty again? What good is a light put under a bushel?

I don't care if there's a COVID-19 kill rate of 90%; the Church must be open. I don't care if hospitals shut down; the Church should still be open. The gospel of Jesus Christ being preached is the most important thing on planet Earth. Going to church is an essential part of Christianity. God brought people together in the early Church. They met in a building and prayed, and the building shook. They weren't meeting at home; they defied the Roman government when they were told they couldn't meet. This is not a game; this is warfare.

As many as 11 Kenyan Christians were killed in a bus attack by a Somali-based radical Islamic terrorist group. According to a Christian persecution watchdog group, police said a group of armed men ambushed a bus traveling from Nairobi to Mandera, a region on the border of Somalia with a large ethnic Somali population. According to a witness who spoke with the local news outlet, assailants separated 11 Kenyan workers from the ethnic Somali passengers on the bus. How did the Christian report this? The witness said, "One of the Muslim men gave me Somali Muslim attire, and when they separated us, I went to the side of the Muslims. They killed all the Christians on board. I dressed up like a Muslim and hid with the Muslims. And immediately we were told to get on the bus. As the locals were getting back into the bus, the non-locals who were left behind were fired upon with gunshots. Two of the victims were evangelical teachers, and three were Catholics.

When the jihadists came, they didn't say, "Now, how many of you are Baptist? How many of you believe in the pre-Tribulation Rapture? How many of you believe that the baptism of the Holy Ghost is evidenced by speaking in other tongues?" People from all denominations should fight together. Al-Shabaab has continuously expressed its desire to eradicate Christians from the world. In fact, I was in South Africa when one of those attacks happened, and I read the quote of the victim's wife.

"The jihadist said with a sword to his head, 'Say there is no God but Allah and Muhammad is his messenger.' Instead, he said, 'Our father, which art in Heaven, hallowed be thy name.'"

The wife spoke with such a glowing face you'd have thought he won the Super Bowl. She said, "We'll see him again on the other side. We're so proud of him."

What are you willing to die for?

There are four things you need to realize:

Number one: The early Church gave their lives.

Number two: Many Christians now must give their lives.

Number three: Western Christians seem to do whatever it takes to stay alive and keep peace with the government at all costs.

Number four: If obeying the government all the time was a commandment in scripture, why did the apostle Paul spend so much time in prison?

> If you refuse to take up your cross and follow me,
>   you're not worthy of being mine. If you cling to
>   your life, you will lose it.
>
> — MATTHEW 10: 38-39

"If you cling to your life, you will lose it." When was the last time anybody read that from an American pulpit? You must *"take up your cross"* in order to call on the name of Jesus. You carry it, or you won't make it to Heaven. Jesus said that. I wouldn't be surprised if many people from the Western Church stand before God on judgment day saying, "Oh Lord, we did miracles in your name and cast out devils in your name" and hear, "depart from me; I never knew you, you workers of iniquity." They have denied the faith to save their own lives. They must repent and pick up their crosses. They must quit trying to make peace with the Devil. Some pastors abandoned the flock of God and left them with nowhere to go for prayer, and nowhere to

go for healing. Leaders are supposed to give their people an example to follow. The early disciples left everything to follow Jesus, but you would be hard-pressed to find a Western Christian that has left anything to follow Him.

Bishop David Oyedepo has the largest church on the planet. When his church was smaller, Muslims came to destroy it. What did he do? He didn't move; he said to all his people, "Everybody that has a rifle, bring it. If you don't have a rifle, bring a machete." They stood, 3,000 strong, in front of the church the day the Islamic insurgents said they would come. When the Muslims crested the hill and saw them standing there, the insurgents turned around and ran the other way.

The Devil wants to manipulate you and get you to give up. He has no plan to stop a Christian who won't lie down. Demon-possessed people did not get to override what God said in the Bible. You don't get a different standard. Thank God for the freedoms we have, but if the day comes where the Devil wants to press you, stand and fight. If you get into the river of compromise, you'll go all the way downstream. You'll end up doing whatever it takes to be a state-accepted church. Defy the Devil.

> Then Jesus said to his disciples, "If any of you wants
> to be my follower, you must give up your life,
> take up your cross and follow me. If you try to
> hang onto your life, you will lose it. But if you
> give up your life for my sake, you'll save it."
>
> — MATTHEW 16:24-25

> "And they have defeated him by the blood of the
> Lamb and by their testimony. And they did not
> love their lives so much that they were afraid to
> die."
>
> — REVELATION 12:11

How do you reconcile this with scriptures about God's protection? What did Shadrach, Meshach, and Abednego say to King Nebuchadnezzar?

> Shadrach, Meshach, and Abednego replied, "O Nebuchadnezzar, we do not need to defend ourselves before you. If we are thrown into the blazing furnace, the God whom we serve is able to save us. He will rescue us from your power, Your Majesty. But even if he doesn't, we want to make it clear to you, Your Majesty, that we will never serve your gods or worship the gold statue you have set up."
>
> — DANIEL 3:16-18

So, at last, the king gave orders for Daniel to be arrested and thrown into the lion's den. The king said to him, *"May your God, whom you serve so faithfully, rescue you."* A stone was brought and placed over the mouth of the den. The king sealed the stone with his own royal seal and the seals of his nobles so no one could rescue Daniel. Then the king returned to his palace and spent the night fasting. He refused his usual entertainment and couldn't sleep at all that night. The king got up very early the next morning and hurried out to the lions' den. When he got there, he called out in anguish, "Daniel, servant of the living God! Was your God, whom you serve so faithfully, able to rescue you from the lions?"

> Daniel answered, "May the king live forever! My
>> God sent his angel, and he shut the mouths of the
>> lions. They have not hurt me, because I was
>> found innocent in his sight. Nor have I ever done
>> any wrong before you, Your Majesty."
> The king was overjoyed and gave orders to lift
>> Daniel out of the den. And when Daniel was
>> lifted from the den, no wound was found on him,
>> because he had trusted in his God.
>
> — DANIEL 6:21-23 (NIV)

Our God is able to deliver us, but even if He doesn't, we'll never bow. God will keep me protected. I'll be happy to rot in prison before I ever compromise to do what "they" say to do. Stand with Jesus! There's an old saying from the preachers in Africa: "The man who says, 'If I die, I die' never dies." The only ones that got roasted by the fire were the ones that complied; the only ones that got eaten by lions were the ones that complied. What are you willing to die for?

Number one: I am willing to die to keep my obedience and gather together. More often, as we see the coming of the day of the Lord, I'm willing to die over someone telling me I can't go to church.

Number two: I'm willing to die to publicly preach the gospel. Most nations don't ban churches, but they have "anti-conversion laws," portraying evangelism as coercive and converts as victims. My jurisdiction is the entire world.

Number three: I will obey the command to pray for and minister to the sick and dying. When they say you're not allowed to pray for people right now, fight back.

Number four: I will never renounce Christ or the Word. What if they make it illegal to speak in tongues like in Syria? Nobody, not even an angel in Heaven, can override the Bible.

And they overcame him by the blood of the Lamb
and by the word of their testimony, and they did
not love their lives to the death.

— REVELATION 12:11 (NKJV)

How do you overcome the Devil? With the blood of the Lamb, the word of
your testimony, and willingness to die for God. All you ever hear about is
the blood of the Lamb and the Word of your testimony. You notice that the
third one is always conveniently left out. There's a power and bravery that
rises up in people's hearts that tells the Devil, "You can't manipulate me.
I've given up my life."

Our insurance company called us during the pandemic and threatened to
drop us if we kept meeting. I told them to drop me! Do you think I care
about insurance and lawyers? We used to sing a song when we were little
kids: "Take the whole world but give me Jesus."

You're going to end up with two different types of Christians. You're going
to have ones that celebrate the accolades they're given by the government,
and you're going to have others who celebrate like Paul. Paul's list of
accomplishments included being in prison, being beaten, and being ship-
wrecked several times without food. His accolades did not include a
Masters of Divinity or Doctorate of Divinity. Paul wrote, *"I bear on my
body the scars that show I belong to Jesus."* If Paul always followed the
law, how did he get those marks?

2

CONSPIRACY THEORIES, THE ANTICHRIST, AND AGENDA 2030

FIGURATIVE OR LITERAL?

When COVID broke out, there were two kinds of ministers. There were ministers like Johnson Suleman, who in April stated that the government will keep everybody locked down until a vaccine comes out, and they're not going to allow citizens to re-enter society without the vaccine. Then the other ministers mocked the former and called such ministers conspiracy theorists while turning their own churches into vaccination centers.

> Then I saw another beast coming out of the earth. He
> had two horns like those of a lamb, but he spoke
> with the voice of a dragon. He exercised all the
> authority of the first beast and he required all the
> earth and its people to worship the first beast
> whose fatal wound had been healed. He did
> astounding miracles, even making fire flashed
> down to earth from the sky while everyone was
> watching. And with all the miracles he was

allowed to perform on behalf of the first beast,
he deceived all the people who belong to this
world. He ordered the people to make a great
statue of the first beast, who was fatally
wounded and then came back to life. He was
then permitted to give life to this statue so that it
could speak. Then the statue of the beast
commanded that anyone refusing to worship it
must die.

He required everyone —small and great, rich and
poor, free and slave —to be given a mark in the
right hand or on the forehead. And no one could
buy or sell anything without that mark, which
was either the name of the beast or the number
representing his name. Wisdom is needed here.
Let the one with understanding solve the
meaning of the number of the beast, for it is the
number of a man. His number is 666.

— REVELATION 13:11-18

The difference between how I cover Bible prophecy and how people who get into trouble cover Bible prophecy is the difference between taking God's Word figuratively or literally. We'll focus on what you can take literally from the book of Revelation and stay away from speculation. An example of what may be open to speculation is asking what the two horns represent when the above passage says there's a beast that comes up out of the earth, and he has two horns. But what can you take literally that is not open to speculation? You can be certain the beast required everyone to receive a mark in their right hand or on their forehead and no man could buy or sell without that mark. You can take literally that rich or poor, free or slave; nobody was exempt.

One of the excuses people have for keeping out of Revelation is that they get confused when they read it. But if you stick with what's clearly said, you will get a lot out of it. There's a blessing for getting into the book of Revelation and reading it to the churches.

> Blessed is he who reads and those who hear the
> words of this prophecy, and keep those things
> which are written in it; for the time is near.
>
> — REVELATION 1:3 (NKJV)

CONSPIRACY THEORIES

Some evangelical leaders say Biblical prophecy is all conspiracy theories. However, it is impossible to believe the Bible is infallible and at the same time not believe there are powerful men with hidden agendas looking to control the population. Perhaps the leaders who call Bible prophecy a conspiracy theory bought Bibles that have the book of Daniel ripped out. Were there leaders that gathered in a back room to make laws to make sure Daniel lost everything and was killed? Yes. Is that the last time you see something like that in the Bible? No. It's impossible to believe the Bible and not believe some powerful people want to control the world. The Bible describes an antichrist spirit operating in the political realm, which we'll discuss later in this chapter.

If I had told you two years ago that what you saw on "The Simpsons" regarding a vaccination requirement to participate in society was actually going to happen, you would have thought I was nuts. I wouldn't seem crazy now. When my dad preached on this stuff in the 1980s, and he said you're going to have to get a mark on your hand or forehead to be able to participate in society, he sounded insane. How could you even do that in 1980? How could you even do that in 1990? But now, it doesn't take any faith to believe the Bible; it's all out in the open. Do you think all of these technologies, like facial recognition, are being instituted by good-hearted people that just want peace and safety? Or do you think it's part of an agenda for total population control? You would have to be one happy-go-lucky, naive son-of-a-gun to believe there are no ulterior motives.

Kansas

Consider the things that were openly discussed during the beginning of the pandemic: we heard that states were going to force you to download an app and keep your phone with you so they could keep track of who you were near, using Bluetooth technology. Then they would know if you had been exposed to someone who tested positive for COVID, and you would be automatically forced to quarantine. If implemented, this technology would allow the government to get its hand in everything. If they shut churches down, then you couldn't also meet privately because they'd be able to see that there were 40 people gathered at a house via this technology. They'd be able to see it and shut it down. In fact, that has already happened in Canada. However, you don't have to worry about it because the government doesn't have the infrastructure to pull something like that off. But they are working towards it, and according to the Bible, they will get it done.

People say, "That sounds like a conspiracy theory." So, you don't believe the government has ever conspired to do anything against a group of people? Read a little Native American history and see what the US government did to them. Look at the Tuskegee experiment. Poor black people in Tuskegee, Alabama, were told they were receiving a vaccine when they were actually injected with syphilis. They were given syphilis by the government to study untreated syphilis in black populations. President Bill Clinton officially apologized to the black community for what happened.

Consider the prophecy that no man will be able to buy or sell without a mark on their hand or on their forehead; the Bible prophesied a cashless society. I was surprised they didn't hop on that in April and May of 2020 when people were concerned about surface transmission of COVID-19. I was in a store in Texas, and all I had on me was cash, and they said they didn't take cash, so I couldn't make the purchase. You can see that everything is going according to what the Bible prophesied.

Currently, in Sweden, there are already about 3,000 people who are inserting microchips under their skin so they will not have to carry cash, IDs, and key cards. The chips are the size of a grain of rice and are being used for anything from gym passes to train tickets. One of the leading

36

companies responsible for implant technology is called Dsruptive Subdermals, and their CEO is Hannes Sapiens Sjoblad. Do you know how much revenue the government loses from untraceable purchases through cash? If your restaurant's 'cash only,' the government just has to take your word for how much your sales are, but if you go cashless, they'll get taxes on everything. Cash allows you to operate privately. Once you take cash away, and everything's done by a microchip implant, they can boot you out of living by turning your chip off just like they can boot you off a social media platform for violating community policy.

Maybe you don't mind a vaccine passport, but do you think your vaccination status is the only thing they will track? If you go to check out somewhere, they scan your passport and say, "Oh, your taxes aren't paid. You can't buy groceries until your taxes are paid." What if they scan you and say, "It says you have diabetes, so the government doesn't permit you to buy ice cream." I can see them saying that because you have diabetes, there's a chance that consuming ice cream could cause a spike in your sugar, therefore causing a drain on our healthcare. So, for the country's good and public health, they can't allow you to buy ice cream. Everything about you would be tracked by the government. It will move to complete control because power-hungry people will stop at nothing.

You might ask how people who know the Word of God can agree to a vaccination passport or a microchip implant. The answer is that those who agree with it don't really know the Word of God. America is a thorn in the side of globalism because many people here have had the Word of God preached to them. However, America has a young generation that has not had the Word preached into them. If we don't immediately ramp up the preaching of God's Word, we'll lose the nation. That's why I am writing this book.

As a Christian, you must question everything your good-hearted parents taught you about allegiance to your government and government leaders. If anybody starts heading down the path that Revelation 13 describes, you need to resist them with every fiber of your being. While I'm sure some people developed COVID-19 policies for good reasons, the Bible tells you where things are going and gives you a responsibility to stand against it. In 2014, or even 2019, if someone predicted a vaccination requirement to participate in society, no one would believe them. Proof of vaccination or a negative test is now required to travel, attend events, and sometimes to go to the grocery store. I don't oppose the vaccine on medical grounds but on biblical grounds. The fact that in 92 AD, John wrote that you would need a mark in your hand or in your forehead to buy or sell, and you can now see the world headed in that direction, you can be sure the Bible is infallible and the inspired word of God. There are things you have to be willing to die for.

According to the book of Revelation, there are five political agendas of the Antichrist.

Number one: A one-world government. *He was given authority to rule over every tribe and people and language and nation.* (Revelation 13:7)

Number two: A one-world military capable of enforcing the Antichrist's edicts.

Number three: A one-world religion. In Revelation 13, the Antichrist makes a statue and commands all the world's people to worship it.

Number four: A one-world money system. This will be the dissolution of individual national economies. *No one could buy or sell anything without that mark, which was either the name of the beast or the number representing his name.* (Revelation 13:17)

Number five: A one-world ruler whom the Bible calls the Antichrist. Christ is not Jesus's last name; Christ means "anointed one," so the Antichrist will operate against the anointing.

Anytime you see a denomination, a government, or a politician going down one of these paths, or all of these paths, you know you're dealing with somebody who does not operate in the spirit of Christ. Supporting a world with no borders and the dissolution of cash is a sign of the antichrist mentality.

RACING TOWARD AGENDA 2030

Now, let's deal with Agenda 2030. To better examine Agenda 2030, I want to share two interesting Bible prophecies regarding the fig tree and the end of the church age.

> "Now learn a lesson from the fig tree. When its
> branches bud and its leaves begin to sprout, you
> know that summer is near. In the same way,
> when you see all these things, you can know his
> return is very near, right at the door. I tell you the
> truth, this generation will not pass from the scene
> until all these things take place. Heaven and
> earth will disappear, but my words will never
> disappear."
>
> — MATTHEW 24:32-35

This scripture tells us there's a limitation on how long God can delay the Rapture of the Church and the Second Coming. The rebirth of Israel is the fig tree budding again, this started a countdown from May 14th, 1948. Look at what's happened since that day. The world was the same from the time of Christ until the early 1900s; people traveled almost the same way, people had horses and then came the rapid ramp-up of technology. This had to happen because all those Bible prophecies would have been impossible to fulfill otherwise.

This leads us to the second Bible prophecy regarding the church age. From creation to Abraham was 2,000 years exactly. From Abraham to the birth of the church, exactly 2,000 years. I find it very interesting that about 2033 or 2034 will be the 2,000-year mark of the third age, and the United Nations has announced Agenda 2030. According to an interview I conducted with Pro-Family NGO United Nations Representative, Mattea Merta (now co-host with me on Check the News), Agenda 2030 is a plan of action instituted in 2015, building off the Millennium Development

Goals. Currently, there are Sustainable Development Goals in place to achieve Agenda 2030. Within Agenda 2030, there are 17 goals and 169 targets. The overall goal of Agenda 2030 is to transform the world. Its preamble states that it is a plan of action for all people, and all the planet, to achieve prosperity. It states that all countries, and all stakeholders, have to act in a collaborative partnership and implement this plan. It all sounds nice, but it is blatant socialism.

In a recent interview with Mattea, she went through the 17 objectives, comparing what they are proposed to be to what they actually are:

1. No Poverty—meaning socialism
2. Zero Hunger—meaning socialism
3. Good Health and Wellbeing—proposing universal health coverage, meaning socialism
4. Quality Education—including comprehensive sexuality education, essentially indoctrination
5. Gender Equality—meaning sameness between the sexes
6. Clean water and sanitation—while there are multiple layers to this goal, it is essentially socialism
7. Affordable and Clean Energy—the doing away with all fossil fuel, the institution of global carbon tax, and the Paris climate accord, meaning socialism
8. Decent Work and Economic Growth—meaning population control
9. Industry Innovation and Infrastructure—essentially restrictions on private property rights, meaning population control
10. Reduced Inequalities—meaning gender studies, i.e. feminist ideologies
11. Sustainable Cities and Communities—meaning population control
12. Responsible Consumption and Production—meaning socialism, communism, and population control
13. Climate Action—this is essentially fear-mongering
14. Life Below Water—this is fear-mongering in terms of climate change amongst current and future populations

15. Life on Land—this has multiple factors, all regarding anything that has to do with being human, private property rights, production, and consumption patterns
16. Peace, Justice, and Strong Institutions—this is the transformation of how governance will be carried out, locally to globally
17. Partnerships for the Goals—this is essentially the doing away of sovereignty

The World Economic Forum (WEF) released a video that tells what the future will look like in accordance with Agenda 2030. This is the World Economic Forum telling you that, in the future, you will own nothing and be happy about it. They're telling you their agenda.

> Now the Spirit speaketh expressly, that in the latter
> times some shall depart from the faith, giving
> heed to seducing spirits, and doctrines of devils;
> Speaking lies in hypocrisy; having their conscience
> seared with a hot iron;
> Forbidding to marry, and commanding to abstain
> from meats...
>
> — 1 TIMOTHY 4:1-3 (KJV)

In the same video, the WEF said Western values will be tested to their breaking point; meaning a press against Christianity. In the words of Mattea Merta, someone I've had on my broadcast plenty of times, the WEF and the UN despise Christianity because it teaches people to put God above government. Christianity tells you that you are not a victim and that work is a gift from God. It's a form of worship for the Christian to do all for the glory of God. Christianity empowers believers to go into their community and be a resource. Mattea explains that Judeo-Christian values are frightening for governments and organizations like the UN or WEF because they want you to solely rely upon them. The end goal for these organizations is a one-world government, and Christians see this for what it is: demonic.

I can discuss all these troubling things while still being happy because I know that for everything the Devil has planned, *God has a counterplan.* God's people operate in a different dimension than the rest of the world. The UN's plan for total population and financial control mirrors what Pharaoh did to God's people in Egypt. They were burdened with work, they weren't paid, and they couldn't own anything. Then God brought them out of Egypt loaded with silver and gold (Psalm 105:37). Without God, all you know is what the Devil has planned, and you have no ability to do anything about it. With God, Jesus destroyed the Devil's power and He raised those that are born again together with Him and seated them in heavenly places, far above all principalities and all powers (Ephesians 2:6). Though we know what the enemy has planned, who cares? If God is for you, nobody can be against you.

The Devil has a financial plan to seize all your property and take away all private ownership, but that is not scriptural. God gave man land as a gift. He didn't give land to governments. Private property is God's idea. Abraham ranched his own cattle. He didn't ask the Canaanites if he could have a food allotment.

God created man to take personal dominion over the earth, subdue it, and then be fruitful and multiply. Every plan against that is against God.

> "Then he ordered, 'Take the money from this
> servant, and give it to the one with the ten bags
> of silver. To those who use well what they are
> given, even more will be given, and they will
> have an abundance. But from those who do noth-
> ing, even what little they have will be taken
> away. Now throw this useless servant into outer
> darkness, where there will be weeping and
> gnashing of teeth.'"
>
> — MATTHEW 25: 28-30

If God is a socialist, why did He have the talent taken from the servant who had one and given to the other servant who had the most? In Matthew 25, the Bible says that even those present objected saying, "But that man already has 10 talents," to which Jesus replied, "Yes, and to he who does well with what he's given, he will be given more and have an abundance. But to he who squanders what he's been given, even the little he has will be taken away." God is not a socialist.

The action plan God gave you is found in Malachi 3. Nothing has changed.

> "I am the LORD, and I do not change. That is why
> you descendants of Jacob are not already
> destroyed. Ever since the days of your ancestors,
> you have scorned my decrees and failed to obey
> them. Now return to me, and I will return to
> you," says the LORD of Heaven's Armies.
> "But you ask, 'How can we return when we have
> never gone away?'
> "Should people cheat God? Yet you have
> cheated me!
> "But you ask, 'What do you mean? When did we
> ever cheat you?'
> "You have cheated me of the tithes and offerings due
> to me. You are under a curse, for your whole
> nation has been cheating me. Bring all the tithes
> into the storehouse so there will be enough food
> in my Temple. If you do," says the LORD of
> Heaven's Armies, "I will open the windows of
> heaven for you. I will pour out a blessing so
> great you won't have enough room to take it in!
> Try it! Put me to the test! Your crops will be
> abundant, for I will guard them from insects and
> disease. Your grapes will not fall from the vine
> before they are ripe," says the LORD of Heav-
> en's Armies. "Then all nations will call you

> blessed, for your land will be such a delight,"
> says the LORD of Heaven's Armies.
>
> — MALACHI 3:6-12

God's tithing and offering program is designed to exempt you from the plans of wicked men who want to make you poor. That's why the Devil fights against tithing with every fiber of his being. You have a choice: you can scorn God's commands like they did in Malachi 3, and like many do today. Or, you can obey. If you obey, God never fails to keep His end of the deal. *See if I won't pour out a blessing that's so great, you'll never have enough room to take it all in.* Who controls the open windows of Heaven? Does the World Economic Forum get a vote? Does the International Monetary Fund get a vote? Do the Democrats get a vote? Do the Republicans get a vote? Does the United Nations have any control over the windows of Heaven? When God decides to bless you, nobody can curse you.

Now that you know this, you need to be born again. You need to be saved because the Bible says that when you are born again, God holds you in His right hand.

> Then those who feared the Lord spoke with each
>   other, and the Lord listened to what they said. In
>   his presence, a scroll of remembrance was
>   written to record the names of those who feared
>   him and always thought about the honor of his
>   name.
> "They will be my people," says the Lord of Heav-
>   en's Armies. "On the day when I act in judg-
>   ment, they will be my own special treasure. I
>   will spare them as a father spares an obedient
>   child. Then you will again see the difference
>   between the righteous and the wicked, between
>   those who serve God and those who do not."
>
> — MALACHI 3:16-18

> The Lord of Heaven's Armies says, "The day of
>   judgment is coming, burning like a furnace. On
>   that day the arrogant and the wicked will be
>   burned up like straw. They will be consumed—
>   roots, branches, and all.
> "But for you who fear my name, the Sun of Right-
>   eousness will rise with healing in his wings. And
>   you will go free, leaping with joy like calves let
>   out to pasture."
>
> — MALACHI 4:1-2

We live in this world, but we're not of this world. If you surrender your life to Christ, He is the only one who controls you. You're safe in His hands.

3

THE FIRE WILL NEVER GO OUT

THE LAST DAYS

The outpouring of the Holy Spirit in the upper room kicked off the last days, and we're living in the final moments. If it's 2,000 years precisely from Adam to Abraham, 2,000 years precisely Abraham to Christ and the birth of the Church, what happens 2,000 after the birth of the Church? Everybody thought Y2K would be a big deal because they said, "Well, now it's 2,000 years since the birth of Christ," but actually it was from the outpouring of the Holy Ghost. The birth of the Church took place around 30-34 AD. I find it interesting that the United Nations and global powers are racing toward an agenda, right at the 2,000-year culmination of the Church age, to bring about a one-world government, one-world monetary system, and total population control.

The Devil knows we're coming to the close of the Church age, and he is pushing his people to build the infrastructure needed to have the one-world government ready to go after the Rapture of the Church takes place.

ONE-WORLD LEADER

That one-world leader will be the Antichrist; he will demand worship of himself. The mark of the beast is not just going to allow you to buy and sell; it will also be a sign of allegiance to the Antichrist.

> Then I saw a beast rising up out of the sea. It had
> seven heads and ten horns with ten crowns on its
> horns. And written on each head were names that
> blasphemed God. The beast looked like a leop-
> ard, but it had the feet of a bear and the mouth of
> a lion! And the dragon gave the beast his own
> power and throne and great authority.
> I saw that one of the heads of the beast seemed
> wounded beyond recovery —but the fatal wound
> was healed. The whole world marveled at this
> miracle and gave allegiance to the beast. They
> worshiped the dragon for giving the beast such
> power, and they also worshiped the beast. "Who
> is as great as the beast?" They exclaimed, "Who
> is able to fight against him?"
> Then the beast was allowed to speak great blas-
> phemies against God, and he was given authority
> to do whatever he wanted for forty-two months.
> And he spoke terrible words of blasphemy
> against God, slandering his name and his
> dwelling — that is, those who dwell in heaven.
> And the beast was allowed to wage war against
> God's holy people and to conquer them. And he
> was given authority to rule over every tribe and
> people and language and nation.

> — REVELATION 13:1-7

America used to be such a strong nation that many taught that the Antichrist would only rule over the European nations. They said there would be no way for an Antichrist to ever rule over the whole world with the American Constitution and Bill of Rights. It would have been impossible to rule over a 1980s United States, but now things are much different.

The new generation of people in this country doesn't care about the Constitution. These people, and some Christians, are happy to do anything the government tells them. They'll shut their churches down and won't re-open until the Department of Health says they can.

In getting filled with the Holy Spirit, you should divorce yourself from the world. I live in the world, but I'm not of the world. You won't catch me posting selfies at a Taylor Swift concert, like some of my 40-year-old friends in the ministry do. I was glad when the media released hateful articles about my having church during Easter 2020. I'm happy the powers of this world don't like me; I'd be nervous if they did. If the women on the View wanted to have me on their show, I'd know I was in trouble. I live in the world, but I don't belong to the world.

The Antichrist will not be a typical political leader because he will demand worship of himself.

> And he was given authority to rule over every tribe
>   and people and language and nation. And all the
>   people who belong to this world worshiped the
>   beast. They are the ones whose names were not
>   written in the Book of Life that belongs to the
>   Lamb who was slaughtered before the world was
>   made.
> Anyone with ears to hear
>   should listen and understand.
> Anyone who is destined for prison
>   will be taken to prison.
> Anyone destined to die by the sword
>   will die by the sword.

> This means that God's holy people must endure
> persecution patiently and remain faithful.
>
> — REVELATION 13:7-10

The Church is mentioned 19 times in Revelation chapters 1 through 3.

> Then as I looked, I saw a door standing open in
> heaven, and the same voice I had heard before
> spoke to me like a trumpet blast. The voice
> said, "Come up here, and I will show you what
> must happen after this."
>
> — REVELATION 4:1

After the previous verse, you never hear the Church mentioned again. If you live a holy life, if you receive Jesus Christ, and keep your garments white and live pure until the coming of the Lord, you're not going to be around for the Tribulation. That's a great motivation to live holy.

> Then I saw another beast come up out of the earth.
> He had two horns like those of a lamb, but he
> spoke with the voice of a dragon. He exercised
> all the authority of the first beast. And he
> required all the earth and its people to worship
> the first beast, whose fatal wound had been
> healed. He did astounding miracles, even making
> fire flash down to the earth from the sky while
> everyone was watching. And with all the mira-
> cles he was allowed to perform on behalf of the
> first beast, he deceived all the people who belong
> to this world. He ordered the people to make a
> great statue of the first beast, who was fatally
> wounded and then came back to life. He was

> then permitted to give life to this statue so that it
> could speak.
>
> — REVELATION 13:11-15

The Antichrist is not going to do tiny miracles. King Nebuchadnezzar was the first person on record in the Bible who had this demon—or perhaps Satan himself—influence him to take over the world. We know from Daniel chapter 3 that Nebuchadnezzar went into Jerusalem, conquered the temple, and ate and drank out of the holy instruments in the temple. Nebuchadnezzar's empire died that day, and every empire that has ever touched Jerusalem since then has died.

For example, the British used to say that the sun never set on the British Empire because it was always daytime somewhere on their own land. The first piece of property the British lost was Israel. You touch Israel, you die.

Nebuchadnezzar was intent on one-world rulership. He went into the temple, just like the Antichrist, and erected a statue that he commanded everyone to worship or else they'd be thrown into a furnace. This will be repeated, just like Babylon the Great all over again.

> He was permitted to give life to this statue so that it
> could speak. Then the statue of the beast
> commanded that anyone refusing to worship it
> must die.
> He required everyone —small and great, rich and
> poor, free and slave —to be given a mark in the
> right hand or on the forehead. And no one could
> buy or sell anything without that mark, which
> was either the name of the beast or the number
> representing his name. Wisdom is needed here.
> Let the one with understanding solve the

meaning of the number of the beast, for it is the
number of a man. His number is 666.

— REVELATION 13:15-18

Then I saw the Lamb standing on Mount Zion and
with him were 144,000 who had his name and
his Father's name written on their foreheads.
And I heard a sound from heaven like the roar of
mighty ocean waves or the rolling of loud thun-
der. It was like the sound of many harpists
playing together.

This great choir sang a wonderful new song in front
of the throne of God and before the four living
beings and the twenty-four elders. No one could
learn this song except the 144,000 who had been
redeemed from the earth. They have kept themselves as pure as virgins, following the Lamb,
wherever he goes. They have been purchased
from among the people on the earth as a special
offering to God and to the Lamb. They have told
no lies; they are without blame.

And I saw another angel flying through the sky,
carrying the eternal Good News to proclaim to
the people who belong to this world —to every
nation, tribe, language, and people. "Fear God,"
he shouted. "Give glory to him. For the time has
come when he will sit as judge. Worship him
who made the heavens, the earth, the sea, and all
the springs of water."

Then another angel followed him through the sky,
shouting, "Babylon is fallen —the great city is
fallen —because she made all the nations of the
world drink the wine of her passionate
immorality."

Then a third angel followed them, shouting,
"Anyone who worships the beast and his statue
or who accepts his mark on the forehead or on
the hand must drink the wine of God's anger. It
has been poured full strength into God's cup of
wrath. And they will be tormented with fire and
burning sulfur in the presence of the holy angels
and the Lamb. The smoke of their torment will
rise forever and ever, and they will have no relief
day or night, for they have worshiped the beast
and his statue and have accepted the mark of his
name."

This means that God's holy people must endure
persecution patiently, obeying his commands and
maintaining their faith in Jesus.

And I heard a voice from heaven saying, "Write this
down: "Blessed are those who die in the Lord
from now on. Yes, says the Spirit, they are
blessed indeed, for they will rest from their hard
work; for their good deeds follow them!"

Then I saw a white cloud, and seated on the cloud
was someone like the Son of Man. He had a gold
crown on his head and a sharp sickle in his hand.

Then another angel came from the Temple and
shouted to the one sitting on the cloud, "Swing
the sickle, for the time of the harvest has come;
the crop on earth is ripe." So the one sitting on
the cloud swung his sickle over the earth, and the
whole earth was harvested.

After that, another angel came from the Temple in
heaven, and he also had a sharp sickle. Then
another angel, who had power to destroy with
fire, came from the altar. He shouted to the angel
with the sharp sickle, "Swing your sickle now to
gather the clusters of grapes from the vines of

53

the earth, for they are ripe for judgment." So the
angel swung his sickle over the earth and loaded
the grapes into the great winepress of God's
wrath. The grapes were trampled in the winepress outside the city, and blood flowed from the
wine press in a stream about 180 miles long and
as high as a horse's bridle.

— REVELATION 14:1-20

The previous verse is where you get the prophecy that blood will flow in the streets during that time of war and the Great Tribulation. This is not going to be a good time to be around. Reading this should motivate you to live holy. You don't want to be left behind, and there will be people left behind. The Bible clearly predicts a one-world ruler and one-world religion, and a false prophet. The Antichrist will have a second character with him, the false prophet. The false prophet is a religious leader who does miracles but points to the Antichrist. This is similar to how John the Baptist pointed to Jesus, except John the Baptist did no miracles. This prophet will also give life to a statue, commanding people to worship the Antichrist.

The Bible says that the Antichrist will go into the temple and claim he is God. He'll defy all gods. The Bible says he'll slaughter a pig in the temple in Israel, and he'll blaspheme every other god there is.

Back when Islam looked like it was going to take over the whole world, people asked, "Is the Antichrist going to be a Muslim?" No, he won't be because the Bible says the Antichrist will defy every other religion.

> Now the Spirit speaketh expressly, that in the latter
> times some shall depart from the faith, giving
> heed to seducing spirits, and doctrines that come
> from devils.
> Speaking lies in hypocrisy, having their conscience
> seared with a hot iron;
> Forbidding to marry....
>
> — 1 TIMOTHY 4:1-3 (KJV)

THE TWELFTH MAHDI

You might find yourself asking how a one-world religion could ever succeed with the massive size of Islam. I have always wondered how Muslim people will accept a universal religion. However, it's actually in their own writings that there will come a 12th Mahdi, who will be a reformer of Islam. In Islamic eschatology, Jesus's descent will be in the midst of wars fought by al-Mahdi, known, in Islamic eschatology, as the Redeemer of Islam. According to Islamic tradition, Jesus will descend against the Antichrist and his followers. He will say a prayer behind al-Mahdi, joining him in his war against the Antichrist. They believe Jesus will kill the Antichrist, and everyone will join him, and there will be one community of Islam. Islamic eschatology prophesies that Christ will return alongside somebody who will usurp Muhammad and reform Islam with Christ. The Devil knows Bible prophecy, so he already established that Islam expects two figures to rule the world.

Between Islamic eschatology and the growing apostasy of the Christian Church, the stage is set for the coming one-world religion.

THE GREAT FALLING AWAY

How will a one-world religion succeed with the size of the Christian Church? There will be a great falling away. The Bible says there will be a turning against Biblical marriage between a man and a woman. There will be a shift from different definitions of marriage to forbidding marriage entirely. It will progress from an openness to new ideas against God, accepting them, and then mandating allegiance to ideas contrary to the Bible.

> ...forbidding to marry, and commanding to abstain
> from foods which God created to be received
> with thanksgiving by those who believe and
> know the truth. For every creature of
> God is good, and nothing is to be refused if it is
> received with thanksgiving; for it is sanctified by
> the word of God and prayer.
>
> — 1 TIMOTHY 4:3-5 (NKJV)

The LGBT rights movement is a perfect example. It has progressed from the idea that what two people do in the privacy of their own bedroom is nobody's business, to the idea that you're an evil person if you don't support children being able to change their gender.

The Bible says it won't stop there. Marriage will be forbidden, along with eating meat. Some people, under demonic influence, are buying up farmland to make sure cattle are not produced; this is all in fulfillment of Bible prophecy. You should eat a steak today, and when you pray, say, "Thank you, Father, that I'm not a globalist." The Bible says it comes from the Devil; this is why I'm not a vegan. I'm not saying all vegans are under demonic influence, but forbidding people to eat meat is a doctrine of devils.

> Now the Spirit expressly says that in latter times
> some will depart from the faith, giving heed to
> deceiving spirits and doctrines of demons...
>
> — 1 TIMOTHY 4:1 (NKJV)

To depart from Pittsburgh, first, I must be in Pittsburgh. I can't depart from a place I've never been. Therefore, when the Bible says many will depart from the faith, it doesn't mean sinners will get more wicked. It means people in the holy faith, as passed down by the Holy Ghost through the apostles in the Word of God, will leave the faith and heed seducing spirits and doctrines that come from devils. Has that already happened? Of course, it has.

It's interesting that churches known for accepting people, no matter what they believe, are still opposed to people who believe in the baptism of the Holy Ghost and speaking in other tongues. If there's a United Methodist church in town, they would be happy to have me preach if I was married to a man, which is specifically forbidden in the Bible, but they will not have me if they find out that I'm filled with the Holy Ghost and speak in other tongues. There is and will be a great falling away.

One of the cardinal tenants of the Christian faith is found in Jesus' words: *I am the way and the truth and the life. No one comes to the Father except through me.* (John 14:6) Not *a* way, *a* truth, and *a* life, but *The* Way. There's no other bridge from unholy man to holy God except through the cross of Jesus Christ. Still, the Catholic News Agency, under the new Pope, put out a video saying it doesn't matter how you contact God or through what channel; we're all children of God, and we need to come together. Additionally, in an interview with his longtime atheist friend, Eugenio Scalfari, Pope Francis claims that Hell doesn't exist. This is all a fulfill-ment of Bible prophecy.

Smith Wigglesworth said that every false religion claims there is no such thing as sin and denies eternal punishment in Hell. As soon as you give yourself over to seducing spirits, that's the two things they seduce you out of. They will convince you there's no such thing as sin, "You just had an issue, you were born gay, your alcoholism's a disease that's in your genes. There's no sin; nobody has sin." NO, the Bible calls it sin. It's wicked, and it has to be driven out of you by the power of the blood of Jesus. The second thing they'll convince you of is that there is no Hell, "We're all children of God, I think in the end, everything works out." It's one thing if you're a sinner who doesn't believe in the Bible, but it's another thing if you're a religious leader, like the Pope, and say there's no such place as Hell. In that case, you and Jesus see things differently.

About sin and Hell, the Pope purportedly said, "…those who do not repent and cannot therefore be forgiven disappear. Hell does not exist; the disappearance of sinful souls exists." He can't back that up with scripture, he pulled that out of Satan's rear. Nobody can write their own book or amend the Bible.

> And if anyone removes any of the words from this
> book of prophecy, God will remove that person's
> share in the tree of life and in the holy city that
> are described in this book.
>
> — REVELATION 22:19

The Pope's statement is not a denial of the 2,000-year-old teaching of the Catholic Church; it's a denial of the Bible, of final judgment. I'm not anti-Catholic, I'm anti-every-Christian-group that turns its back on the Bible. To anyone reading this who has never heard of being against anything, God the Father was against things in the Old Testament. Jesus was against things in the gospels, and the apostles, under the power of the Holy Ghost, opposed things in the New Testament. I'm not bringing this up to bash the Catholic Church. But when you question how there can be a one-world ruler when there are a billion Catholic people, you can see that Catholics will not fall away and follow a different religion; they already have.

There's a great man of God I know, and he and his wife made a pretty startling statement to me. They said, "We've seen people who are Christians fall into trouble, then recover from nearly everything, including homosexuality, affairs, alcoholism, and drug addiction. The only thing we've never seen anyone recover from is the subversion of the Word of God." The Bible is an anchor; if you do away with it, you're finished, and you have no foundation. A building with no foundation has its destruction guaranteed.

"Anyone who listens to my teaching and follows it is
wise, like a person who builds a house on solid
rock. Though the rain comes in torrents and the
floodwaters rise and the winds beat against that
house, it won't collapse because it is built on
bedrock. But anyone who hears my teaching and
doesn't obey it is foolish, like a person who
builds a house on sand. When the rains and
floods come and the winds beat against that
house, it will collapse with a mighty crash."

— MATTHEW 7:24-27

And I saw a great white throne and the one sitting on
it. The earth and sky fled from his presence, but
they found no place to hide. I saw the dead, both
great and small, standing before God's throne.
And the books were opened, including the Book
of Life. And the dead were judged according to
what they had done, as recorded in the books.
The sea gave up its dead, and death in the grave
gave up their dead. And they were all judged
according to their deeds. Then death and the
grave were thrown into the lake of fire. This lake
of fire is the second death. And anyone whose
name was not found recorded in the Book of Life
was thrown into the lake of fire.

— REVELATION 20:11-15

Jesus said, "There was a certain rich man who was
splendidly clothed in purple and fine linen. And
who lived every day in luxury. At his gate lay a
poor man named Lazarus who was covered with
sores. As Lazarus lay there longing for scraps

from the rich man's table, the dogs would come
and lick his open snores.

"Finally, the poor man died and was carried by the
angels to sit beside Abraham at the heavenly
banquet. The rich man also died and was buried.
And he went to the place of the dead. There, in
torment, he saw Abraham in the far distance with
Lazarus at his side.

"The rich men shouted, 'Father Abraham, have some
pity! Send Lazarus over here to dip the tip of his
finger in water and cool my tongue. I'm an
anguish in these flames.'

"But Abraham said to him, 'Son, remember that
during your lifetime you had everything you
wanted, and Lazarus had nothing. So now he's
here being comforted and you are in anguish.'"

— LUKE 16:19-25

Hell is a place of torment. Anyone who believes and is baptized will be saved. Anyone who refuses to believe will be damned, Jesus said that. Jesus did not say they will disappear.

"And besides, there's a great chasm separating us.
No one can cross over to you from here, and no
one can cross over from us to there."

— LUKE 16:26

They can light every candle in Rome for you after you die, but there is no crossing over. Life is the space of time God gives a man to repent before he crosses into eternity. *What shall it profit a man, if he shall gain the whole world, and lose his own soul? Or what shall a man give in exchange for his soul?* (Mark 8:36-37) That's life. In all your getting, get Christ. In all your learning, learn the Bible. When you come to the end of your life, you are going to stand before God. Don't let any Pope confuse you, don't let any skinny-jean-wearing preacher confuse you, don't let any talking statue confuse you. You will stand before Jesus Christ and either meet Him as your savior or as your judge; don't let anyone tell you differently.

> "Then the rich man said, 'Please, Father Abraham, at
> least send him to my father's home. For I have
> five brothers, and I want him to warn them so
> they don't end up in this place of torment.'"
>
> — LUKE 16:27-28

Isn't it interesting that a man who never had time for God his whole life, when he was in Hell, suddenly wanted to be an evangelist? He thought, "tell my family about this place. If I can't get out, make sure they don't come." This is the great falling away.

SIGNS OF AN APOSTATE CHURCH

Number one: They have little or no regard for the Bible. They'll say things like, "Let me just read a scripture real quick, or some religious person will get mad at me." I'm not talking about Catholics, I'm talking about charismatic churches that don't care one iota about the Bible. You don't hear anything about the Bible. Instead, they talk about the dream they had last night or play a popular movie to learn some principle from it. There's no scripture and no Bible preaching. Get out of places like that.

Number two: They don't believe Jesus is the only door to the Father. Jesus did not come down and die on the cross for fun. What an insult to the sacrifice of Christ! Mohammad did not die for me. Buddha did not die for me. In fact, they demanded their followers die for them. Jesus died for me; He became a sacrifice for my sin. Apart from Jesus, there is no remission of sin. There is a Heaven, and the only people who will be there are those who overcome, not those who bow and keep their mouths shut to fit in with American media. They can take you to where Mohammad's bones are.

They can take you to where Buddha's buried. Jesus is *alive*, and He lives forevermore. Ask yourself how often you hear the name of Jesus in your church. *I am the way, the truth, and the life. No one can come to the Father except through me.* (John 14:6 NLT)

Number three: They have light regard for sin. If you hear something like, "I mean, we all sin," you're listening to a demon. You're listening to a doctrine of demons. An apostate church will say things like, "We all sin. How many know we all sin? Let's all just pray the sinner's prayer." No, I'm not praying the sinner's prayer. I'm not a sinner. I was a sinner, but the blood of Jesus cleansed me of all unrighteousness, and now I'm a new creature. I'm born again. Romans 6:14 says sin shall not have dominion over you, so don't just pray the sinner's prayer after you're saved. If you're going to do that, then why don't you throw on a black robe and a white collar and we'll just go to confession every week. There will be people in the pulpit this Sunday that have given multiple STDs to members of their congregation. They will go to Hell. They could repent, but they don't repent. I don't care how well they preach, and I don't care how awesome their revelation is; they're demonized. The Church has accepted this behavior because they've been lulled to sleep by apostasy. Who taught the Church that sin is normal? Jesus made a trip to Earth from Heaven to destroy the power of sin, and if you stand up there and make people comfortable in it, you will answer to God. It's in your best interest to run from a Christian leader that makes you comfortable with something that'll cost you an eternity in Hell. Sin shall not have dominion over you.

Number four: They have light regard for the baptism of the Holy Ghost and the gifts of the Spirit. *They will act religious, but they will reject the power that could make them godly.* (2 Timothy 3:5) The Greek word here for power is *dunamis*, meaning Holy Ghost power. In the same way Christians have become comfortable in churches that make allowance for sin, they get comfortable in churches with a light regard for the power of God. They make little jokes about getting slain in the spirit and about tongues. They'll make excuses for not having anybody speaking in tongues in their church. They'll say things along the lines of, "Well, I've talked to our pastoral staff, and they told me they believe in that, and this actually used to be a church where words were given, and they used to pray for the sick, but now they just feel like there's a lot of people in the congregation who aren't ready for that." Make no mistake, they backslid. They're apostate: they have a form of godliness but have rejected the power of the Holy Ghost. There's a problem if your kid has to go to summer camp to get the baptism of the Holy Ghost, and there's a problem if you have to go on a retreat to get healed. The power of God in the book of Acts was on display in the gathering of the Church, and anything else is a bastardized substitute form of godliness. They deny the power.

Consider these denominations that have opened their door to homosexuality, Presbyterian Church USA, United Methodist Church, etc., do they pray in other tongues? Do they lay hands on the sick? No, they don't. As soon as you start backing away from the Spirit of God and His power, you start receiving the spirit of the world and its power. Even in some Full Gospel churches, when someone speaks in tongues, the pastor says, "We've heard something today that many of us might not be familiar with." Why aren't you familiar with the Holy Spirit? Why do you have to give an apology every time there's a demonstration of the Holy Spirit? These churches will make an excuse and say, "Well, there are visitors here that don't know." Let me tell you something; if the Holy Ghost comes in demonstration, the Holy Ghost will speak to the people. It's a sign to the unbeliever. Peter didn't get up and apologize; he said, "What you're hearing today was spoken of by the prophet Joel," and it pricked their hearts. Imagine Pentecost Sunday in a Full Gospel church where the pastor makes an apology for something one Sunday a year, that should be happening every Sunday. If you're never at a place where the Word of the Lord is declared by the Spirit, then there's nothing over your life that God can confirm. Ezekiel prophesied to the bones. Someone has to say it for God to come behind it; that's how it works.

> "And I will give you the keys of the Kingdom of
> Heaven. Whatever you forbid on earth will be
> forbidden in heaven, and whatever you permit on
> earth will be permitted in heaven."
>
> — MATTHEW 16:19

If you're at a place where there's no flow of the Holy Ghost in the meeting, and nothing's ever declared over your life by the Spirit, then there's nothing for God to confirm. Prophecy matters. The gifts of the Spirit weren't given for nothing; they bring profit. We know Satan has these evil things planned for the Church in the last days. But we also know God has the opposite plan; a mighty move of His Spirit, an end-time church, and a remnant Church that will not bow to the world but will stand up against the worldly spirit regardless of the consequences. *I will pour out my Spirit on all flesh. (Acts 2:17)*

A REMNANT REVIVAL

Though many shall depart from the faith, there will be an explosion of the power of the Holy Ghost in the remnant bride of Christ's Church that will shake the earth one more time before Jesus comes back. The auditoriums, indoor arenas, and stadiums worldwide were not built for those sports teams. God has used the money of heathen people and organizations to build buildings large enough to house the crowds that will hear the gospel of Jesus Christ and receive the power of the Holy Ghost before the end comes.

BE ENCOURAGED!

Don't allow the backsliding of others to discourage you. Jesus said, these things must happen, but you make up your mind that you're not joining them and that you're going to be on fire for God. The fire must never go out. In Matthew 25, you see five that were wise and five that were foolish. They all had the fire burning, but five fell asleep and let the fire go out. The other five brought extra oil and kept the fire burning. Make sure that you're living on fire from today forward for God. I don't want less fire; I want more fire. I don't want less Holy Ghost; I want more Holy Ghost. I don't want less passion; I want more passion. I don't want less boldness; I want more boldness. I pray you are filled with the Holy Ghost; receive what you require to live in this wicked age, to not join them, to carry power, to tread on serpents and scorpions and subdue them under your feet.

4

AN ATTACK FROM WITHIN

THE PLANNED DEMOLITION OF THE CHURCH

> Don't you remember that I told you about all this
> when I was with you. And you know what is
> holding him back, for he can be revealed only
> when his time comes. For this lawlessness is
> already at work secretly, and it will remain secret
> until the one who is holding it back steps out of
> the way. Then the man of lawlessness will be
> revealed, but the Lord Jesus will slay him with
> the breath of his mouth and destroy him with the
> splendor of his coming.
>
> — 2 THESSALONIANS 2:5-8

The Bible teaches that something is restraining the Antichrist. God is not on the Devil's clock. The Devil runs on God's clock. The Devil doesn't get to pick when the Tribulation begins or when the Antichrist takes power. This is why you can look throughout history and see that the Devil has always needed an Antichrist at the ready, because God is the one that pulls the strings, not Satan.

What is standing in the way of the Antichrist being revealed and doing what he wants to do? Finis Dake, in his Bible commentary, says the hinderer of lawlessness is this:

1. It's something that's already known.
2. It now hinders lawlessness.
3. It is strong enough to prevent the revelation of the Antichrist.
4. It will hinder lawlessness until it is removed from the earth.
5. It's called 'he.'
6. It will be removed from the earth before the second advent.
7. It will not be here when Christ comes to destroy the Antichrist.

That leaves only three things that the hinderer could be: Governments, the Church, or the Holy Spirit.

The hinderer of lawlessness must be that which will be taken out of the world *before* the Antichrist can be revealed.

Will governments be taken out of the world? No, because Antichrist reigns over many kingdoms. Look at Daniel 7:24 and Daniel 11:40-45. Numerous kings will reign over the rest of the earth when the hinderer of lawlessness is removed.

Will it be the Holy Spirit? No. For He will be here all through the Tribulation and forever. Multitudes will be saved by the Holy Spirit during the Tribulation, just as now.

It is *the Church*. It will be raptured before the Antichrist comes. This is the only valid option among the potential hinderers of lawlessness that will be removed from the earth. Yet, it's being called 'he.' Some may question this saying, "Isn't the church the bride of Christ?" They think the hinderer of lawlessness is the Holy Spirit, but the only argument used to prove the Holy Spirit is the hinderer of this passage is the pronoun 'he.' Some people are confused and believe the church could not be referred to as "he" because it is the bride of Christ, because the church is spoken of as a virgin woman, and because it is referred to by feminine pronouns.

But on the contrary, the Church is not referred to by feminine pronouns, it is never symbolized as a woman and is never called the Bride of Christ. The Church is called a man in Ephesians 2:15 and Ephesians 4:13-15. The Church is called the Body of Christ according to 1 Corinthians 12, Ephesians 1, and Colossians 1. Because Christ is a man, it would not be proper to compare his body to that of a woman, a lady, a virgin, or a bride, and is not referenced by feminine pronouns. Since the Church is called a man and the Body of Christ, who is a man, the Church can be referred to by the pronoun 'he.'

The Church is the only one of the three hinderers of lawlessness taken out of the world. We must therefore conclude that 'he', or the hinderer of lawlessness in 2 Thessalonians 2:7, must refer to the Church being taken out of the world at the Rapture.

The Antichrist will be destroyed seven years later by Christ at His second advent.

> Now the Holy Spirit tells us clearly that in the last
> times some will turn away from the true faith;
> they will follow deceptive spirits and teachings
> that come from demons. These people are
> hypocrites and liars, and their consciences are
> dead.
>
> — 1 TIMOTHY 4:1-2

The Bible says the marks of the last days are not just things happening in the world, but in the Church; there will be a "great falling away." This is not talking about the world getting more wicked because you can't fall away from a place you've never been. This is talking about many that were once in the faith leaving it. In fact, let's read another scripture. Go to Matthew 25. Matthew 24 is where the disciples ask Jesus in verse 3, "What signs will there be to signal your return," and Christ gives all the signs. Look at the parable He shares immediately afterward.

> "Then the kingdom of heaven will be like ten brides-
>   maids who took their lamps and went to meet the
>   bridegroom. Five of them were foolish, and five
>   were wise. The five who were foolish didn't take
>   enough olive oil for their lamps, but the other
>   five were wise enough to take along extra oil.
>   When the bridegroom was delayed, they all
>   became drowsy and fell asleep.
> "At midnight, they were roused by the shout. 'Look,
>   the bridegroom is coming! Come out and meet
>   him!'
> "All the bridesmaids got up and prepared their
>   lamps. Then the five foolish ones asked the
>   others, 'Please give us some of your oil because
>   our lamps are going out.'
> "But the others replied, 'We don't have enough for
>   all of us. Go to a shop and buy some for
>   yourselves.'
> "But while they were gone to buy oil, the bride-
>   groom came. Then those who were ready went in
>   with him to the marriage feast, and the door was
>   locked. Later, when the other five bridesmaids
>   returned, they stood outside calling, 'Lord! Lord!
>   Open the door for us!'
> "But he called back, 'Believe me, I don't even know
>   you!'
> "So you, too, must keep watch! For you do not know
>   the day or hour of my return."

> — MATTHEW 25:1-13

Dr. Willard Cantelon, who was a very smart man, said, "If you take this literally, of the 10 that originally had the fire, 5 let the fire go out and were locked out. 50% of the church that once was ready, that is the mystery of immorality, the Bible calls it, works in the earth and it makes people's hearts grow cold. If you take what Jesus said literally, 5 out of 10 who were once ready will not be ready."

There's no question in my mind that the Church is the restrainer of not only the Antichrist personally, capital 'A', but also the antichrist's spirit, small 'a', that's in the world. And, of course, it's not speculation. 1 Timothy tells you it'll happen.

There's an attempt of the Devil to, like a cancer, destroy the Church from the inside. The two factors fueling the planned demolition from within the Church that we will cover in this chapter are Critical Race Theory and George Soros.

CRITICAL RACE THEORY

Jordan Peterson, a Professor of Psychology at the University of Toronto for Prager University, describes Critical Race Theory as the indoctrination of young minds with resentment-ridden ideology[1]. He says that the people pushing Critical Race Theory have made it their life's mission to undermine Western civilization itself, which they regard as corrupt, oppressive, and patriarchal. They claim all truth is subjective, all sex differences are socially constructed, and Western imperialism is the sole source of all third-world problems. They're the postmodernists pushing progressive activism at a college near you. Peterson explains that the goal of these postmodernists is to have all the classic rights of the West considered secondary to diversity, equity, and inclusion. For example, one of these Western rights they aim to subvert is the freedom of speech. In a recent video for Prager U, Jordan Peterson goes on to say…

> "The postmodernists refuse to believe that people of goodwill can
> exchange ideas and reach consensus. Their world is instead a
> Hobbesian nightmare of identity groups warring for power. They

don't see ideas that run contrary to their ideology as simply incorrect. They see them as integral to the oppressive system they wish to supplant and consider it a moral obligation to stifle and constrain their expression. They won't acknowledge that capitalism has lifted up hundreds of millions of people out of poverty. Finally, postmodernists don't believe in individuals. You're an exemplar of your race, sex, or sexual preference. You're also either a victim or an oppressor. No wrong can be done by anyone in the former group, and no good by the latter. All these concepts originated with Karl Marx, the 19th-century German philosopher. Marx viewed the world as a gigantic class struggle, the bourgeoisie against the proletariat, the grasping rich against the desperate poor. But wherever his ideas were put into practice, in the Soviet Union, China, Vietnam, and Cambodia, to name just a few, whole economies failed, and tens of millions were killed. We fought a decades-long cold war to stop the spread of those murderous notions. But they're back in the new guise of identity politics."

We know universities are liberal, so what does this have to do with the demolition of the Church? Well, when Bible colleges that train ministers kept increasing their tuition, making it so students couldn't afford to attend, the students needed federal student loans. To qualify for federal student loans, the college has to be accredited. To be accredited, many of your professors must have an advanced degree, even at a Bible college. The only places you can get advanced degrees are liberal, post-modern types of universities. This cycle planted these ideals into ministers, which in turn, got these ideals into the church.

I saw it happen personally. I went to Bible college from 1998-2002. Halfway through my time in Bible college, they decided they wanted to get federal student loan money, meaning they wanted to get accredited. When the Bible college started to pursue accreditation, almost all of the old ministers that trained us—guys that had been in the ministry 40 years or 50 years—were fired and replaced with people that had Master's degrees and PhDs. Many of these new professors had never been in the ministry, and they mocked miracles and the baptism of the Holy Ghost. This happened at a Pentecostal school, by the way. If you are going to a full-gospel accredited Bible college right now, that's actually a red flag because to get accredited, you have to have professors that are produced from this cycle we discussed.

According to a Pew Research Center survey[2] reported in 2015, from 2007-2014, most US Christian groups grew more accepting of homosexuality, with an acceptance rate of 54%. I'd love to see the updated numbers; if the acceptance rate was 54% in 2014, I guess it could be 61% in 2021. This poll was published 7 years ago when gay marriage was newly legalized. How is this information related to what we just talked about? As you start having university professors from liberal hellhole universities training the next generation of ministers, there's no wonder why there's an erosion of belief in Bible morality.

Do you ever wonder why the teenagers that leave your church and go to Bible college come back with nose rings, sit in the back pew with their arms crossed, and eventually stop attending church? Federally-recognized accredited Bible colleges are the public school of ministry training. You can attend full gospel Bible colleges with Black Lives Matter groups on campus and pro-Democrat party initiatives. If the college receives federal money, it's a major red flag. This may cost me a few friends, but I suggest you avoid sending your child to federally-recognized, accredited Bible colleges. However, there is a private ministry training accreditation that's not recognized by the federal government, which is a green light for me.

Would you allow people who hate you, your family, and your God to cook your dinner? Of course not. Then why would you let them raise your children? Get out of the system as much as you can. I understand that everybody can't live in Northern Saskatchewan with no electronics or in the desert of Arizona in a trailer with a satellite dish and a generator. I get it. But as much as possible, withdraw from the system that takes your children from pure, innocent babies and turns them into pornography-addicted, mind-medication-requiring lunatics on their way to Hell. Get them in a

Christian school and a Holy Ghost church that lays hands on people, anoints with oil, and prays for the sick.

> They will act religious, but they will reject the power
> that could make them godly. Stay away from
> people like that!
>
> — 2 TIMOTHY 3:5

The word here for "power" is *dunamis,* meaning the power of the Holy Ghost that could make them godly, so they will reject the power that could make them godly. The Bible says to have nothing to do with them, not to oppose them, not to yell at them, and not to make social media posts against them. It says to not join yourself to people who reject the power of the Holy Ghost.

I hear pastors say, "We take our church to so-and-so's conference. They're not spirit-filled, but we like some of the ideas and leadership that they have in." Then everybody comes back with the same haircut that the conference leader had, so don't tell me it doesn't influence you. Don't tell me it doesn't slowly turn your church into a powerless place. I have not seen any churches where the leadership started to get enamored with non-Holy Ghost leadership and start following them, and then didn't have their church turn into a place void of the spirit. I'm not against ministries that don't see eye-to-eye with me doctrinally on the gifts of the Spirit and the baptism of the Holy Ghost, but I don't knit my ministry to them and thus lose the power that's the secret to thriving in the final hours of time.

It will only be a short time before the first charismatic church performs a gay marriage and becomes an LGBTQ-inclusive church. If you already have +30% of the people who attend your church accepting lawlessness, it will go from being here-and-there to being a groundswell.

What happens when everybody who is now 60 years and older is dead, and the new crop coming up believes like the world? You'll have boards of churches made up of those children who say, "Why are we opposing that stuff? What is it, 1800? We should accept what the Bible specifically says to condemn because, after all, the Bible was translated by people that read their own cultural thoughts into the text. It's not inspired."

The Bible *is* inspired; stay with the Bible.

One of the side effects of having liberal professors in Bible colleges is they don't produce ministers anymore. How many people graduate from full-gospel Bible colleges and go into the ministry? There are essentially no people even looking to go into the ministry.

I'd like to know how many recent graduates from the University of Valley Forge or Lee University went into full-time ministry compared to how many ministers these schools produced in 1970. People aren't even studying for the ministry there.

A certain kind of church service calls people into the ministry. But it's not the 75-minute smoking light show you typically see on a Sunday. It's most certainly not done by people who think the Bible is a construct of Western society.

Major denominations like the Assemblies of God have 30,000 ordained ministers, but only a few hundred are under the age of 30. Therefore, even the churches that look strong are headed down the same road as the Methodists and everyone else.

Director of the National Institutes of Health, Dr. Francis Collins, on CNN encouraged white evangelicals who are reluctant to get the COVID-19 vaccine to do so. He said, "I think God works through science in cases like this."

The first two words he said were, "I think." Let me tell you something, I don't give a crap what you think. I care what the Bible says. As soon as you start chipping away at the authority of scripture, you're in a dangerous place. Where did this new generation of people come from, who think their thoughts are not only on par with God's thoughts but have the authority to override God's thoughts? If you're a minister, go in the other direction; be bold.

I'm tired of being on social media and seeing guys that used to be full of the Holy Ghost looking for spiritual fatherhood from people who don't believe in the demonstration of the Holy Ghost. You become like those you're around, so stay with people who are on fire. Go to war against anything that produces lukewarmness, indifference, or deadness in your spirit.

GEORGE SOROS

Now that you see how accreditation weakens the church through training ministers with critical race theory, let's look at the destructive influence of leftists such as George Soros and others. Well-funded evangelicals, supported by George Soros-funded pro-immigrant groups, are rewriting the Bible; they are redefining how American Christians understand concepts like immigration, borders, and nations. Critical race theory in universities has made its way to Bible translators. They actually believe the Bible is not inclusive enough and it needs to be retranslated to make it more inclusive. I believe you should just read it in the original language and then translate it accordingly.

According to a September 23, 2019 article in Pulpit and Pen[3]...

> "...these groups manipulate evangelicals through pious-sounding platitudes and exploitations of biblical ignorance. Surveys show evangelicals don't read their Bibles very often. It makes it easier to deceive them.
> Most people in the pews aren't aware of the ancient languages or the historical context of antiquity. It is this general ignorance that allows a Southern Baptist PhD to claim that Jesus was a so-called "illegal immigrant." As we've pointed out, Jesus wasn't an illegal immigrant. Jesus wasn't a refugee. Applying these modern legal terms to a pre-modern world is theological malpractice. However, even if we were to do it, Jesus wouldn't meet the legal definition spelled out in international law.
> Yet, this is how Big Eva [Big Evangelicalism] operates. They are

fast and loose with the facts. Narrative trumps detail. And after all, Snopes would rate these progressive claims true in spirit if not in fact.

What won't surprise anyone paying attention is that well-funded groups and Big Eva itself are promoting new ways to view Scripture. More often than not, the lens of identity politics is coloring how so-called conservative evangelical leaders and professors interpret and teach the Bible.

It threatens how we translate the Bible and it also threatens how we understand the Bible... There is special knowledge for special people based on their skin color according to this view. This is the rise of ethnic Gnosticism and it's dangerous.

According to scholars, including one panel discussion held at Southeastern Baptist Theological Seminary, one's ethnicity and background "speaks into how we read the text." Here are two explicit examples from the panel discussion about how ethnic values are distorting a plain understanding of the text.

Professor Miguel Echevarria explained how his ethnic background shaped his reading of the Bible:

"I noticed as a Cuban, a Latino, my background was really shaping the things I was seeing in the text."

A Wheaton College professor Dr. Danny Carroll attacked the idea that there would be only one, universal biblical theology:

"In a meeting where I was being questioned by the head of an institution," Dr. Carroll said during the panel, "We were talking about Latin American Evangelical Theology. Here was the question, (listen, you guys will appreciate this), 'Isn't there only one biblical theology?' And I said, 'Well, who gets to decide what that is? Americans?' Someone is making decisions about what can be in and what can be out. The text should be making those decisions."

"This isn't a battle over the inspiration of scripture nor sufficiency, but the doctrine of the perspicuity of scripture is the Bible clear and understandable by all or only some based on their skin color or sex. Do some believers possess special knowledge or does the Holy Spirit illuminate all? Is one's level of oppression the true arbiter of one's understanding of the biblical text?

"Charles Hodges declared,"The Bible is a plain book."

The belief that one's oppression score gives someone special insight into the text is dangerous. It overturns the evangelical commitment to the clarity of the Scripture. As *Smalcald Articles and the Form of Concord* declared of the Scriptures, "That they are sufficiently perspicuous to be understood by the people, in the use of ordinary means and by the aid of the Holy Spirit, in all things necessary to faith or practice, without the need of any infallible interpreter."

These individuals from Wheaton are chipping away at the inerrancy of scripture, claiming that scripture has been interpreted by whatever culture it was translated in. If you heard that a pastor has a doctorate from Wheaton, idiots would be impressed, but now after reading this, one will say, "yikes." Everything is backward. By the way, Wheaton allows drinking on campus now. There are Pentecostal Bible colleges where the worship teams play Michael Jackson cover songs for school dances. But of course, they didn't have the dances in 2020 or 2021 because of COVID. They have totally secularized holy institutions.

I'd rather have a Bible translation composed by translators who are experts in the original language and capable of rendering those ancient texts in the best English. While I'm on the topic, you can group the passion translation with the other garbage translations that are just somebody's idea of what the Bible should say. What an insult to Scripture to just make it say what you think it should say! Who cares what you like? Is it to the original God-inspired text? If it's not, burn it.

Affirmative action and or racial quotas for Bible translation committees are terrible ideas. However, that is what identity politics does. It divides based on race, it divides on sex; it divides. It's only a matter of time before we see the first Bible with transgender people on the translation committee, which should make an interesting translation of the book of Leviticus.

George Soros funds the Open Society Foundation. This is similar to how you won't see a rich person directly funding someone running for a political position. Instead, they use a corporation or a nonprofit, and they pour their money into that organization which then gives the money to the political candidate. This is what's happening in Christianity right now. George Soros funnels billions of dollars to fund the Open Society Foundation, working towards dissolving the sovereignty of nations, particularly the United States, and to fund the Evangelical Immigration Table.

The Washington Post [4]recently reported that a minister told Nancy Pelosi, "America is better for your prophetic leadership." Prophetic means Holy Ghost inspired, which her leadership is clearly not. Why do you have high-profile leaders in the church selling out to push vaccines or making their church a vaccination center? Or siding with Nancy Pelosi and calling her a prophetic leader? It sometimes serves the Evangelical Immigration Table, funded by George Soros. Shocker. Can you see it now? When you wonder why your favorite high-profile preacher starts making comments in favor of gay marriage or telling you that you need to get the vaccine, now you know why.

You can see where people get their funding from, and you can see they have to bark to their masters. Their masters are wealthy left-siding people who invest billions of dollars into evangelical organizations and people that promote LGBTQ and transgender interests.

An example of this is the Hobby Lobby lawsuit from 2012. Hobby Lobby challenged the 2012 Patient Protection and Affordable Care Act because they would have been required to provide contraceptives and abortions to their employees, which violated their beliefs as Christians. The group that gathered signatures against Hobby Lobby, demanding they provide contraceptives to employees, and held a vigil outside of the headquarters after Hobby Lobby won the lawsuit, was a left-funded "Christian" group called Faithful America.

In 2020, Faithful America, a pro-choice Christian group, opposed a Supreme Court Justice nominee who was confirmed pro-life. Why? I just traced for you in print where their funding comes from. Whenever you see a minister on CNN or MSNBC promoting the LGBTQ agenda and mass vaccination, check to see what boards they sit on. Then check who the boards of those organizations receive their funding from, and it will all make sense.

The plan is to make the Church look like a so-called right-wing hate group and make the pro-LGBTQ, pro-open borders, pro-abortion heretics appear to be the Church. Thanks to this funding, preachers of the past won't be considered preachers anymore; they'll be considered anti-LGBTQ, hate-mongering bigots.

> Now the Holy Spirit tells us clearly that in the last
> times some will turn away from the true faith;
> they will follow deceptive spirits and teachings
> that come from demons.
>
> — 1 TIMOTHY 4:1

WHAT DO YOU DO?

First, know God's plan to stop this: *I will pour out my Spirit on all flesh (Acts 2:17).* Jesus is the head of the Church, and you can't usurp His leadership. You can have all the funding in the world, but you can't usurp Christ. God has a plan to counter this, and this is why if you understand Bible prophecy correctly, it's never depressing. Some teach Bible prophecy like it's all about the Devil's plans, like it's just the Devil doing his thing. God has a plan in the last days. God has an end-time agenda, and the chief of that agenda is laid out in the Bible in Acts 2:17. God's plan is revival, which will destroy the enemy's plans.

Second, what can you do now that you know this? I hate when people teach on this topic and just say that we need to pray. No. There's action you can take. Even the way they say we need to pray is not intended to break this stuff; instead, they say things like, "Well, you know that the Lord will just keep us safe." No, we have dominion over all the power of the Devil. Take action.

Wherever you are, close both eyes and lift both hands. Pray this from your heart:

> "Father, in Jesus' name, destroy in me all lukewarmness and all complacency. Give me fresh fire, that my fire may never go out. When you return, find me full of faith and full of the Holy Ghost. In Jesus' name, Amen."

5

THE ANTICHRIST

THE ANTICHRIST SHALL COME, EVEN NOW

> Dear children, the last hour is here. You have heard
> that the Antichrist is coming and already many
> such antichrists have appeared. From this we
> know that the last hour has come.
>
> — 1 JOHN 2:18

The previous scripture says, *"You have heard that the Antichrist"* with a capital "A," referring to the Antichrist. It also says, *"You have heard that the Antichrist is coming and already many such antichrists have appeared,"* using a lowercase "a", regarding an antichrist spirit. The King James Translation says it like this: *Little children, it is the last time: and as ye have heard that antichrist shall come, even now are there many antichrists; whereby we know that it is the last time.*

Now concerning how and when all this will happen, dear brothers and sisters, we don't really need to

write you. For you know quite well that the day
of the Lord's return will come unexpectedly, like
a thief in the night. When people are saying,
Everything is peaceful and secure," then disaster
will fall on them as suddenly as a pregnant
woman's labor pains begin. And there will be no
escape.

But you aren't in the dark about these things, dear
brothers and sister, and you won't be surprised
when the day of the Lord comes like a thief. For
you are all children of the light and of the day;
we don't belong to darkness and night. So be on
your guard, not asleep like the others. Stay alert
and be clearheaded. Night is the time when
people sleep and drinkers get drunk. But let us
who live in the light be clearheaded, protected by
the armor of faith and love, and wearing as our
helmet the confidence of our salvation.

—1 THESSALONIANS 5:1-8

Now, dear brothers and sisters, let us clarify some
things about the coming of our Lord Jesus
Christ and how we will be gathered to meet
him. Don't be so easily shaken or alarmed by
those who say that the day of the Lord has
already begun. Don't believe them, even if they
claim to have had a spiritual vision, a revelation, or a letter supposedly from us. Don't be
fooled by what they say. For that day will not
come until there is a great rebellion against God
and the man of lawlessness is revealed—the
one who brings destruction. He will exalt
himself and defy everything that people call
god and every object of worship. He will even

84

sit in the temple of God, claiming that he
himself is God.

— 2 THESSALONIANS 2:1-4

Don't you remember that I told you about all this
when I was with you. And you know what is
holding him back, for he can be revealed only
when his time comes. For this lawlessness is
already at work secretly, and it will remain secret
until the one who is holding it back steps out of
the way. Then the man of lawlessness will be
revealed, but the Lord Jesus will slay him with
the breadth of his mouth and destroy him by the
splendor of his coming.

This man will come to do the work of Satan with
counterfeit power and signs and miracles. He
will use every kind of evil deception to fool
those who are on their way to destruction,
because they refuse to love and accept the truth
that would save them. So God will cause them to
be greatly deceived. and they will believe all the
lies. Then they will be condemned for enjoying
evil rather than believing the truth.

As for us, we can't help but thank God for you, dear
brothers and sisters loved by the Lord. We are
always thankful that God chose you to be among
the first to experience salvation—a salvation that
came through the Spirit who makes you holy and
through your belief in the truth. He called you to
salvation when we told you the Good News; now
you can share in the glory of our Lord Jesus
Christ.

— 2 THESSALONIANS 2:5-14

Paul wrote that the Antichrist will be the man of lawlessness, but that spirit is already at work secretly in the world. He also wrote that it will become public when he who is restraining it steps out of the way, the Church. When the Church steps out of the way, the man of lawlessness will come into the public. The main point I want you to take away from the previous scriptures is that there will be an actual Antichrist, and the spirit behind the Antichrist and his governmental structure is already at work in secret.

WHO IS THE ANTICHRIST?

Number one: The Antichrist will be a human possessed and empowered by Satan. It's not a figurative character, it's not a government. Don't listen to people who make the Bible an allegory or a metaphor. Don't listen to people who say things like, "Well, the word 'cloud' refers to people several times in the Bible, so when it says that Christ will return in the clouds, maybe it means that he's actually already returned in us." That's how people who are missing brain cells talk. The Bible says in Acts 1:11, "... *someday he will return from heaven in the same way you saw him go!"* Was there a literal Christ? Yes. Was Christ an idea that came into the world that helped bring salvation? No, he was a man. God who put on flesh and blood and bones and died in our place. In the same way, the Antichrist will not be just an idea. The Antichrist will be a person, a politician, and a one-world ruler. Here's a good rule-of-thumb; if you have ideas about Bible prophecy that nobody in the 2000-year history of the church has ever believed or ideas that church fathers wrote against, change your doctrine. Otherwise, you'll end up being a lunatic.

Number two: The Antichrist will be a man and will be referred to as "he."

Number three: The Antichrist will likely be a homosexual.

> And the king shall do according to his will; and he
>> shall exalt himself and magnify himself above
>> every god, and shall speak marvelous things
>> against the God of gods and shall prosper till the
>> indignation be accomplished: for that that is
>> determined shall be done.
> Neither shall he regard the God of his fathers, nor
>> the desire of women. nor regard any god: for he
>> shall magnify himself above all.

> — DANIEL 11:36-37 (KJV)

Daniel is prophesying about the Antichrist. When I was a kid, my father preached that the Antichrist would likely be a homosexual, and I would say, "Dad, how could a homosexual ever be a political ruler?" Things have changed so quickly that you might have forgotten that President Obama was anti-gay marriage when he ran for president. In 1996, a governor in New Jersey was married with children, and it came out that he had a homosexual affair. When he announced that he was gay, he was immediately forced to step down. If they found out you were homosexual, you were out of politics. So, when my father preached that according to Daniel 11:37, the Antichrist will likely be homosexual, that sounded insane. That's another testament to Bible prophecy because now, if you're a homosexual in politics, not only is it a plus, it makes more people vote for you because, apparently, you're a bigot if you don't support gay marriage.

Number four: The Antichrist will glorify sin. When you see people running for public office on platforms promoting what the Bible calls gross sin, abominations to God, they're operating in the antichrist spirit.

Number five: According to Daniel 9:27, the Antichrist will enter the temple in Jerusalem on at least one occasion.

> "The ruler will make a treaty with the people for a
>> period of one set of seven, but after half this
>> time, he will put an end to the sacrifices and

offerings. And as a climax to all his terrible deeds, he will set up a sacrilegious object that causes desecration, until the fate decreed for this defiler is finally poured out on him."

— DANIEL 9:27

Number six: The Antichrist will be a conqueror.

I looked up and saw a white horse standing there. Its rider carried a bow, and a crown was placed on his head. He rode out to win many battles and gain the victory.

— REVELATION 6:2

They worshiped the dragon for giving the beast such power, and they also worshiped the beast. "Who is as great as the beast?" they exclaimed. "Who is able to fight against him?"

— REVELATION 13:4

Number seven: He'll be a fierce-looking man and have an imposing countenance. The Antichrist will be lovely to look at; he will not be a dementia-ridden geriatric.

"At the end of their rule, when their sin is at its height, a fierce king, a master of intrigue, will rise to power."

— DANIEL 8:23

And of the ten horns that were in his head, and of the other which came up, and before whom three

> fell; even of the horn that had eyes, and a mouth
> that spake very great things, whose look was
> more stout than his fellows.
>
> — DANIEL 7:20 (KJV)

Number eight: The Antichrist will hate the God of Abraham, Isaac, and Jacob.

> Then he opened his mouth in blasphemy against
> God, to blaspheme His name, His tabernacle, and
> those who dwell in heaven.
>
> — REVELATION 13:6 (NKJV)

Number nine: He's commonly called the Antichrist, but he's also referred to in scripture as "the beast."

Number ten: Antichrist will have a partner called the false prophet, found in Revelation 13:13-14.

Number eleven: He will display miraculous powers.

> The coming of the lawless one is according to the
> working of Satan, with all power, signs, and
> lying wonders…
>
> — 2 THESSALONIANS 2:9 (NKJV)

Number twelve: The Antichrist will have authority over all people.

> And it was given unto him to make war with the
> saints, and to overcome them: and power was
> given him over all kindreds, and tongues, and
> nations.
>
> — REVELATIONS 13:7 (KJV)

Number thirteen: The Antichrist will resurrect from the dead.

> I saw one of his heads as if it had been slain, and his
> fatal wound was healed. And the whole earth
> was amazed and followed after the beast; they
> worshiped the dragon because he gave his
> authority to the beast; and they worshiped the
> beast, saying, "Who is like the beast, and who is
> able to wage war with him?"
>
> — REVELATION 13:3-4 (NASB95)

He's Anti-Christ; everything Christ did in redemption, the Antichrist will do in the demonic. He suffers a fatal head wound and resurrects so the entire world can see. At that point, people receive him as a god, not just a political leader.

Number fourteen: The Antichrist will control the economy.

> It also forced all people, great and small, rich and
> poor, free and slave, to receive a mark in the
> right hands or on their foreheads, so that they
> could not buy or sell unless they had the mark,
> which is the name of the beast or the number of
> its name.
>
> — REVELATION 13:16-17 (NIV)

Number fifteen: The Antichrist will be full of boasting.

> And the king shall do according to his will; and he
>   shall exalt himself, and magnify himself above
>   every god, and shall speak marvelous things
>   against the God of gods, and shall prosper till the
>   indignation be accomplished: for that that is
>   determined shall be done.
>
> — DANIEL 11:36 (KJV)

Number sixteen: The Antichrist will gather the world's armies to fight against Jesus when Christ returns. I was always under the impression that when Christ returns, people will realize they missed the boat and wish they had received Him, but the Bible says that's not going to happen. The Antichrist will gather all that have sworn allegiance to him. Unfortunately for them, Jesus is coming back prepared for that. Baby Jesus isn't coming back; mighty Jesus is coming back. He's coming back to judge, to trample the grapes. The Antichrist will gather the world's armies to fight against Jesus.

> Then I saw the beast and the kings of the earth and
>   their armies gathered together to wage war
>   against the rider on the horse and his army.
>
> — REVELATION 19:19 (NIV)

Number seventeen: The Antichrist loses and is thrown into the lake of fire.

> And I saw the beast, and the kings of the earth, and
>   their armies, gathered together to make war
>   against him that sat on the horse, and against his
>   army.
> And the beast was taken, and with him the false

> prophet that wrought miracles before him, with
> which he deceived them that had received the
> mark of the beast, and them that worshipped his
> image. These both were cast alive into a lake of
> fire burning with brimstone.
>
> — REVELATION 19:19-20 (KJV)

That's who the Antichrist will be. Sorry if you were under the impression that I was going to accuse someone of being the Antichrist.

HOW TO SPOT AN ANTICHRIST POLITICIAN

How do you know if a politician is operating in the antichrist spirit? The most important thing is to know what the Bible says and understand Bible prophecy. As a Christian, if you don't know Bible prophecy, you're easily duped into fighting about the Democrat and Republican parties. If you're still prophesying about Biden and Trump, you don't know what's happening. This isn't about Trump. This isn't about Biden. This is about how everything will come under a one-world system. If you don't know the Bible, and you just see Republican vs. Democrat, you'll end up voting for the people who have the antichrist spirit because you don't even know what it is. One of the things that will mark this hour is a time of great deception.

> He will use every kind of evil deception to fool those
> on their way to destruction, because they refuse
> to love and accept the truth that would save
> them. So God will cause them to be greatly
> deceived, and they will believe these lies.
>
> — 2 THESSALONIANS 2:10-11

Christians will vote for politicians with pro-abortion, pro-transgender children's rights (the ability for a child to get a sex change without notifying the parents) platforms because they're ignorant of Bible prophecy. But the Bible says that we're not children of the night, we live in the light. We know these things by the Word. Pro-abortion candidates are usually anti-gun and anti-Israel. It's a spirit, and that spirit flows in seven directions.

SEVEN CHARACTERISTICS OF ANTICHRIST POLITICIANS

Number one: A politician who operates under the spirit of Antichrist is anti-Israel. God said, "Abraham, I will give this land to you and your descendants forever. I'll bless those who bless you. I will curse those who curse you." Therefore, anyone that looks to undo what God has said is permanent is a devil. Any empire that touches Israel dies. Any politician who touches Israel dies. The Antichrist will be possessed with a desire to attack Israel. Those who operate under an antichrist spirit want to take their land from them. Anytime you spot a politician that wants Israel to give its land away, you're listening to an Antichrist politician.

> "This is what the Sovereign Lord says: At that time
>> evil thoughts will come to your mind. and you
>> will devise a wicked scheme. You will say,
>> 'Israel is an unprotected land filled with
>> unwanted villages! I will march against her and
>> destroy these people who live in such confi-
>> dence. I will go to those formerly desolate cities
>> that are now filled with people who have
>> returned from exile in many nations. I will
>> capture vast amounts of plunder, for the people
>> that are rich with livestock and other possessions
>> now. They think the whole world revolves
>> around them!' But Sheba and Dedan and the
>> merchants of Tarshish will ask, 'Do you really
>> think the armies you have gathered can rob them
>> of their silver and gold? Do you think you can
>> drive away their livestock and seize their goods
>> and carry off plunder?'

> "Therefore, son of man, prophesy against Gog. Give
> him this message from the Sovereign Lord:
> When my people are living in peace in their land,
> then you will rouse yourself. You will come from
> your homeland in the distant north with your
> vast calvary and your mighty army, and you will
> attack my people Israel, covering their land like
> a cloud. At that time in the distant future, I will
> bring you against my land as everyone watches,
> and my holiness will be displayed by what
> happens to you, Gog. Then all nations will know
> that I am the Lord."

— EZEKIEL 38:10-16

Number two: They are pro-abortion. God likes children, the more, the better. They love the slaughter of babies. God said to be fruitful and multiply and replenish the earth. An antichrist spirit seeks the destruction of children in the womb. Once they're outside the womb, the antichrist spirit seeks to fill them with hormones and make them a different sex, to mess their minds up. Any politician who wants children to change their sex at six years old, with or without parental notification, is under the influence of demons.

> "I knew you before I formed you in your mother's
> womb. Before you were born I set you apart and
> appointed you as my prophet to the nations."

— JEREMIAH 1:5

Number three: When spotting an antichrist politician, don't get caught up in personality and appearance. If you don't understand this stuff out of the Bible, then you get caught up in personality and appearance. If you find yourself saying, "Oh well, he owns a golden retriever, and I also have a golden retriever. So, I'm going to vote for him." You're a stupid person.

The less Bible you have, the dumber you get. The less Bible you have, the easier you'll be deceived and manipulated. The Bible says a great deception marks this age. The Bible makes you undeceivable, it gives you the spirit of truth to spot a lie.

Number four: Antichrist politicians are anti-family and pro-LGBTQIA+. God created the family before sin entered the world. He didn't say, "Well, now that sin is in the world, people are going to want to have sex. I might as well just make something." No, God ordained the family. The family is God's idea. The husband is the high priest of the home, and his wife is his helpmate; it's a beautiful partnership. When you start hearing people say that a family's whatever you want it to be, you're listening to a demon talking. *In the last days they'll follow doctrines that come from devils.*

> But God shows his anger from heaven against all
> sinful, wicked people who suppress the truth by
> their wickedness. They know the truth because
> God has made it obvious to them. For ever since
> the world was created, people have seen the
> earth and sky. Through everything God made,
> they can clearly see his invisible qualities —his
> eternal power and divine nature. So they have no
> excuse for not knowing God.
> Yes, they knew God, but they wouldn't worship him
> as God or even give him thanks. And they began
> to think up foolish ideas of what God was like.
> As a result, their minds became dark and
> confused. Claiming to be wise, they instead
> became utter fools. And instead of worshiping
> the glorious, ever-living God, they worshiped
> idols made to look like mere people and birds
> and animals and reptiles.
> So God abandoned them to do whatever shameful
> things their hearts desired. As a result, they did
> vile and degrading things with each other's

bodies. They traded the truth of mouth of God
for a lie. So they worshiped and served the
things God created instead of the Creator
himself, who is worthy of eternal praise! Amen.
That is why God abandoned them to their
shameful desires. Even the women turned
against the natural way to have sex and instead
indulged in sex with each other. And the men,
instead of having normal sexual relations with
women, burned with lust for each other. Men did
shameful things with other men, and as a result
of this sin, they suffered within themselves the
penalty they deserved.

Since they thought it foolish to acknowledge God,
he abandoned them to their foolish thinking and
let them do things that should never be done.
Their lives became full of every kind of wickedness, sin, greed, hate, envy, murder, quarreling,
deception, malicious behavior, and gossip. They
are backstabbers, haters of God, insolent, proud,
and boastful. They invent new ways of sinning,
and they disobey their parents. They refuse to
understand, break their promises, are heartless,
and have no mercy. They know God's justice
requires that those who do these things deserve
to die, yet they do them anyway. Worse yet, they
encourage others to do them, too.

— ROMANS 1:18-32

That's God speaking in the New Testament after the resurrection of Christ.
The Bible says they suffered within themselves the penalty they deserve.
There's a penalty for gay sex; anal sex produced AIDS; it didn't just appear
out of nowhere. In fact, AIDS was originally called gay man's disease by
the CDC because there was no record of any heterosexual who had it.

"Since they thought it foolish to acknowledge God, he abandoned them to their foolish thinking and let them do things that should never be done." According to the Bible, there are things you should never do. We don't all sin. If you do, you should stop, or you'll go to Hell. In John 8, Jesus didn't just forgive the woman caught in adultery. He said, *"Neither do I condemn you; go and sin no more."* God gives you the power to live in victory over sin, not for sin to have victory over you.

"Their lives became full of every kind of wickedness, sin, greed, hate, envy, murder, quarreling, deception, malicious behavior, and gossip. They're backstabbers, haters of God, insolent, proud and boastful. They invent new ways of sinning." That's what transgenderism is, a new way of sinning. It doesn't matter if I'm a man and I'm convinced I should be a woman, I cannot turn into one. It takes help from wicked people to give me fake boobs and whatever else they give you. Notice how the Bible correlates this with disobedience to parents. It's dangerous to allow your child to rebel. You have to break a rebellious spirit. *They know God's justice requires that those who do these things deserve to die, yet they do them anyway. Worse yet, they encourage others to do them, too.*

Number five: An antichrist politician is always in favor of disarming the population, starting with gun control and leading to gun registration and confiscation of weapons. Anyone who will not swear allegiance to the Antichrist will be beheaded. As a child, I wondered how they could pull that off in America when everybody's armed; it's hard to behead somebody who has a firearm.

The Second Amendment was made in case a tyrannical government ever rose up against the people, so the people could hold their ground. People ask why somebody would need an AR-15 to go deer hunting, and the Second Amendment was not written in case the deer rise up against us. It was to make sure the populace was as well-armed as the government. That's why you should fight for gun ownership rights with the same passion that you fight against abortion. They all go together.

To all my public-school-educated friends that are reading this who have been taught that America is such a bad place because it has too many guns, remember, you only hear about people killed by private gun owners. You never hear how many people have died because they didn't have access to weapons.

According to the *The Black Book of Communism*,[1] authored by Jean-Louis Panné, et al and published by Harvard University Press and considered one of the best sources on class-genocide in communist regimes, 20 million people were killed in the Soviet Union under Lenin and Stalin; 65 million people were killed under Mao Tse-tung in Communist China; 2 million were killed in Cambodia under Pol Pot; and 150,000 were killed in Latin America, most of the victims in Cuba, ruled by Fidel Castro. Every dictator that has taken guns away has used them against the population. As a Christian, you should fight for personal gun ownership and against abortion with the same passion.

Number six: An antichrist politician glorifies sin. The epitome of this is the Shout Your Abortion campaign. They're not only pro-abortion, but they want you to be proud of your abortion and to share about it. That's brazen blasphemy.

Number seven: They're socialists. They say you need to pay your fair share in taxes, but what's the government's fair share of what you legally earned? You don't owe the government anything. America was founded on rebellion against taxation. America had no federal income tax until 1913, and there were plenty of roads and hospitals. Everything the government says they'll pay for is paid with your money. The money never gets to the people. I'm not interested in the common good. I'm interested in freedom.

Was Jesus a socialist? Did Jesus take the talents from the man that had the most and give them to the one that had the least? No, he actually rewarded the one who produced the most with what he was given and stripped from the one who squandered what he had and gave it to the one who had the most; the exact opposite of socialism.

Though members of the early Church sold all they had and shared things in common, you can't leave out the fact that the church became so poor from doing so, that they had to take a collection. (2 Corinthians 8 and 9). That was never instituted by God.

> "To those who use well what they are given, even more will be given, and they will have an abundance. But from those who do nothing, even what little they have will be taken away. Now throw this useless servant into outer darkness, where there will be weeping and gnashing of teeth."
>
> — MATTHEW 25:29-30

You cannot have a prosperous nation by forcing people that produce goods and services to pay for the penalty of other people's sin. These antichrist politicians hate the Bible because socialism is always predicated on you being a victim. The Bible teaches that you're not a victim; you have dominion no matter where you are right now. The Lord takes the beggar from the dunghill and sets them among princes.

Number eight: Antichrist politicians are anti-national sovereignty because the Antichrist will bring everything under a one-world government and a one-world monetary system. Donald Trump was covered negatively in the news so often because his policies flew in the face of the antichrist system. Nobody asks any questions about Joe Biden because he is going in the flow of the antichrist spirit, or what people who don't know the Bible call globalism.

When you find politicians that campaign or make statements about their hatred for Israel and condemn Israel, pushing for abortion, putting hundreds of millions of US taxpayer dollars into foreign countries to make abortion even more widespread, etc., you know who that politician's master is...the Devil.

6

EIGHT THINGS COVID SHOWED US ABOUT BIBLE PROPHECY

SIGNS OF THE END

The COVID-19 virus showed us how close we are to these astounding prophecies, which five or ten years ago seemed insane.

> Then I saw another beast come up out of the earth. He had two horns like those of a lamb, but he spoke with the voice of a dragon. He exercised all the authority of the first beast. And he required all the earth and its people to worship the first beast, whose fatal wound had been healed. He did astounding miracles, even making fire flash down the earth from the sky while everyone was watching. And with all the miracles he was allowed to perform on behalf of the first beast, he deceived all the people who belong to this world. He ordered the people to make a great statue of the first beast, who was fatally wounded and then came back to life. He was

then permitted to give life to this statute so that it could speak. Then the statue of the beast commanded that everyone refusing to worship it must die.

He required everyone —small and great, rich and poor, free and slave —to be given a mark in the right hand or on the forehead. And no one could buy or sell anything without that mark, which was either the name of the beast or the number representing his name. Wisdom is needed here. Let the one with understanding solve the meaning of number of the beasts, for it is the number of a man. His number is 666.

— REVELATION 13:11-18

As Jesus was leaving the Temple grounds, His disciples pointed out to him the various Temple buildings. But he responded, "Do you see all these buildings? I tell you the truth, they will be completely demolished. Not one stone will be left on top of another!"

— MATTHEW 24:1-2

What Jesus prophesied in Matthew 24 was fulfilled—the temple was plowed under, and this specific order was given by the Roman general, "Don't leave one stone on top of another." It happened exactly as Jesus said it would. The Holy Spirit often gives us early signs to prove later prophecies. An early sign is something that is going to happen soon to give you faith for the things that are going to happen later on.

For example, if I tell a 10-year-old boy, "When you're 21-years-old, you're going to meet a girl in St. Louis, Missouri. Her name is going to be Heather, and you're going to get married," that's hard to believe. But if I then say, "And as a sign, today, when you go home, there's going to be a black puppy waiting at your door, and he's going to become your dog." Then if he comes home and the puppy's there, he will have faith to believe the other things will come to pass. When you hear people make sarcastic comments like, "These people preach out of the Bible like the world's going to end," you know the world as we know it will come to an end. The Bible tells us: *Since everything around us is going to be destroyed like this, what holy and godly lives you should live* (2 Peter 3:11).

> Jesus told them, "Don't let anyone mislead you, for many will come in my name claiming, 'I am the Messiah.' They will deceive many. And you will hear of wars and threats of wars, but don't panic. Yes, these things must take place, but the end won't follow immediately. Nation will go to war against nation, and kingdom against kingdom. There will be famines and earthquakes in many parts of the world. But all of this is only the first of birth pains, with more to come.
> "Then you'll be arrested, persecuted, and killed. You will be hated all over the world because you are my followers."
>
> — MATTHEW 24:4-9

That's a sign of the end times: you'll be hated all over the world simply because you follow Christ. In 2020, all you had to do to get arrested was go to church. A spirit of betrayal and hatred marks the last days.

> And many false prophets will appear and will deceive many people. Sin will be rampant every-where, and the love of many will grow cold. But the one who endures to the end shall be saved. And the Good News of the kingdom will be

> preached throughout the whole world, so that all
> nations will hear it; and then the end will come.

— MATTHEW 24:10-14

No nation has lacked a gospel witness. The Bible doesn't say everybody
will get to hear it; it says it will be preached to all nations.

> "The day is coming when you will see what Daniel
> the prophet spoke about —the sacrilegious object
> that causes desecration standing in the Holy
> Place. (Reader, pay attention!) Then those in
> Judea must flee to the hills. A person on the deck
> of a roof must not go down into the house to
> pack. A person out in the field must not return
> even to get a coat. How terrible it will be for
> pregnant women and for nursing mothers in
> those days. And pray that your flight will not be
> in winter or on the Sabbath. For there will be
> greater anguish than at any time since the world
> began. And it will never be so great again. In
> fact, unless that time of calamity is shortened,
> not a single person will survive. But it will be
> shortened for the sake of God's chosen ones.
> "Then if anyone tells you, 'Look here is the
> Messiah' or 'There he is,' don't believe it. For
> false messiahs and false prophets will rise up and
> perform great signs and wonders so as to
> deceive, if possible, even God's chosen ones.
> See, I have warned you about this ahead of
> time."

— MATTHEW 24:15-25

If there were no Bible prophecy, then you could just be a dumb person that waits until the vaccine's out so you can resume a normal life. You would never think there's an agenda behind the scenes, but the Bible tells you about the things to watch out for. Seeing the prophecies fulfilled thus far gives us faith to know that every part of Bible Prophecy will happen.

WHAT COVID-19 HAS SHOWN

Number one: COVID has shown us that the current generation is ignorant of the economy, law, and history and easily accepts the antichrist system. The Bible says the Antichrist will be a man of lawlessness, and during the pandemic, government leaders violated the law. The government cannot tell the church to shut down, it's illegal. It's a human rights violation to prevent people from practicing their religion. That's not according to the Bible; that's according to the United Nations. Yet, many people said "no problem," while church leaders supported the shutdown; it happened because they're stupid. You never allow the government to cross the bridge into dictating church affairs; that's why I said a generation would have to rise up that's dumb enough to accept the antichrist system. During COVID, we saw that generation exists now. An intelligent generation would not have cooperated with one-world rules telling people they couldn't go to church on Easter. If you're going to allow the government to lock you in your home and give you a little bit of money, you only need to look at history to know it wouldn't end up well. Ask Venezuela or the Soviet Union.

How do you combat stupidity and ignorance? You teach the Word. Not everyone will listen, but some people will get snapped out of it. Those who felt something wasn't right will realize they have a foundation for their beliefs.

Number two: COVID has shown us how close we are to becoming a cash-less society. The Bible says no one will be able to buy or sell without a mark on their right hand or on their forehead. This means—as my father has preached for about 30 years—there will come a cashless society. I was surprised the United States didn't jump on the opportunity to eliminate cash during the height of the pandemic. Some places in Canada did it, along with some countries in Europe. Under the guise of COVID, they could have done away with cash here as well.

Those in the antichrist system want all transactions tracked, which you cannot do with cash. Going cashless would bring in massive amounts of tax revenue because nothing could be done off the books. If my nephew washes my car for me just to be nice, I can say "Thanks" and give him a $100 bill, and that's not traceable. He can claim the income on his tax return if he wants to, but no one would know if he didn't. But without cash, the government would get revenue from everything; they'd know everything you earned and spent. That is total population control.

The mark of the Antichrist also forces a one-world religion; if your church is not approved, there will be no way to give to it. They've already done this in Angola and other countries where they freeze the church's bank account. No credit card companies will do business with religious institutions in those places.

Number three: COVID has shown us that if there's a one-world government, a global entity will replace national and local governments. How is the Antichrist going to have a military system that's able to enforce his edicts globally? This was on full display during COVID when the World Health Organization gave orders, and immediately militaries all over the world mobilized to enforce edicts from a global entity. We saw this in Colombia, Chile, Canada, England, and worldwide. Before this, it seemed impossible, but this was a fulfillment of Bible prophecy. The European Union has already replaced local governments; elected officials in each country do not make the decisions—the EU passes edicts in those countries. This is all fulfillment of Bible prophecy.

Number four: COVID has not only shown us there will be a shift from local officials to global officials, it has also shown how easily this replacement can happen. For example, in most African nations, besides Tanzania, the president or the prime minister just did whatever their global rulers told them to. According to an article in Reuters, on May 3, 2020, Coronavirus test kits used in Tanzania were dismissed as faulty by President John

Magufuli, because he said they had returned positive results on samples taken from a goat and a pawpaw. It's no coincidence that the one prime minister in Africa who exposed the whole Chinese system and their faulty tests was dead within 12 months of doing so.

Number five: COVID has shown us that church leaders will sell out for safety and good standing with the government for the antichrist system to come into power. I would like to know what law *would* have to get passed for a preacher to be willing to get arrested anymore. You heard Christian leaders talk about church, saying things like, "How many know it's not important whether we gather in a building or gather at home?" No, it actually is important. Going to church and meeting with other Christians is important. Do you think it's some side thing we invented that's not actually in the Bible? The pastors you heard saying these things are spineless, weasel sell-outs. If church isn't about a building, then why don't you burn yours down? If it's not important whether we meet together, why'd you spend all that money on a building in the first place? Do you just wet your finger each morning and see which way the wind's blowing and change your doctrine? The same people who shut their churches mocked us for calling such behavior satanic, calling us conspiracy theorists. They call anything they don't want to talk about a "conspiracy." We should meet together more often, not less, as we see the coming of the Lord approaching. *Let us not neglect our meeting together as some people do, but encourage one another, especially now that the day of His return is drawing near* (Hebrews 10:25).

Number six: COVID has shown us a generation of people willing to do anything, to give up any right, to be kept safe. Benjamin Franklin once said, "Those who would give up essential liberty to purchase a little temporary safety deserve neither liberty nor safety."

Number seven: COVID has shown that the government has replaced God in people's lives, which is precisely what needs to happen for the antichrist system to be successfully established. People will look for an earthly ruler and an earthly government to keep them safe, to keep them fed, to keep them protected, and to keep them healed. How many comments did you read about your president, prime minister, or governor not doing enough to stop the virus? Man cannot stop diseases. When the gospel stops being preached, people stop looking at God and start looking to the government.

Replacing God with the government is a dangerous and deadly road. I don't need the government to keep me safe; Jehovah is my protector. I don't need the government to heal me; God is my healer. I don't need the government to provide for me. *"I am Jehovah Jireh; I will provide all your needs."* My God is El Shaddai, the God of more than enough; He supplies everything that pertains to me. I don't need a government leader to help me; I need the government to stay out of my way. Pave the roads, take care of the water supply and infrastructure, but don't meddle in my personal life. Don't tell me who I have to perform marriages for, what I can preach, or when I can hold meetings. The goal of life is not to simply stay alive.

The government has replaced God in many people's lives, including many pastors. God said we're to meet and gather together in church every Sunday, but the government said not to, so to whom will you listen? Do you know what "Jesus is my Lord" means? It means Jesus is my prime minister, Jesus is my president. I cooperate with the country's laws until they infringe on the One to whose Kingdom I belong. If God told you to have church and your president said you can't, and you listen to your president, Jesus is not your Lord. You heard the spineless pastors say, "We need to use wisdom," but they must not have read the part of the Bible that tells us the highest wisdom is to obey the Word of God. God packs churches; the Devil wants to empty churches—they never change roles.

Number eight: COVID has shown us lukewarm Christians who are willing to sell out each other to the government. Pastor Rodney Howard-Browne was arrested in Florida after another pastor turned him in for having church and violating the stay-at-home order. Anytime a church stayed open during the pandemic, you'd see Christians commenting in the church's livestream saying, "I hope they get the virus first. They should build a fence around that church, and those people should all die." *Many will betray and hate each other.* There's a spirit of betrayal and hatred on the loose; make sure it doesn't get in you.

The enemy of my enemy is my friend. If there's another preacher who hates abortion, is standing up for churches being open, and is against the antichrist system, I don't care if he's in my denomination. I don't care if we share the same view on the initial evidence of the baptism of the Holy Ghost. If he believes Jesus is the only way to Heaven and fights against tyranny, he is my friend. *Stop finding reasons to divide yourself from people you're in the same fight with.*

I'm a Full Gospel Pentecostal, and I would go to a Baptist church that was open during the pandemic before I would stay allied to a Full Gospel church that closed. The Pentecostal church might say they believe in healing, and the Baptist church might say they don't. Yet, if the Baptist church is open during a pandemic and the Full Gospel church has shut, which one actually believes in healing? Which one actually believes in God's protection? I heard a Baptist preacher say, "I believe God will keep us safe as we meet." It's not the beliefs people write on paper that matter; it's their actions that show what they really believe. If you're at a Full Gospel church that wears masks and takes temperatures at the door, you're not really at a Full Gospel church. They're backslidden. They're full of unbelief. Did Oral Roberts do temperature checks? Did Kenneth Hagin have a health questionnaire before you were allowed to come to his meeting? Did Lester Sumrall do that? They've betrayed their roots. They're lukewarm and backslidden, and they should repent. Some of you lost Christian friends; they got angry at you because you went to church. Jesus told us that we'd be hated all over the world because we are His followers. But we don't shrink back.

7

ISRAEL, IRAN, RUSSIA, CHINA, AMERICA & ARMAGEDDON

I didn't come up with one original concept for this chapter; I don't do that with Bible prophecy. This is Bible prophecy as established by many, many scholars. If I haven't heard another respected person teach it, I won't teach it.

I used to preach out of these passages concerning prophecy at youth meetings. I would have the youth pastor tell me, "Now listen, our kids don't behave, and they're really wild. They can't pay attention for more than 15 minutes." Yet, when I preached on Bible prophecy, you could've heard a pin drop for two hours. Afterward, people would ask questions for another 90 minutes. This is not lightweight stuff.

ISRAEL

> …When its branches bud and its leaves begin to
> sprout, you know that summer is near. In the
> same way, when you see all these things, you can
> know his return is very near, right at the door. I
> tell you the truth, this generation will not pass

> from the scene until all these things take place.
> Heaven and earth will pass away, but my words
> will never disappear.
>
> — MATTHEW 24:32-35

Everyone listening to Christ knew what He meant when He said, *"when the fig tree buds again."* What nation was Jesus referring to as the fig tree? He was talking about Israel. The generation that sees Israel reborn as a nation will not pass from the scene until all these things are fulfilled.

Israel was reborn as a nation on May 14th, 1948; this was the sign of the fig tree budding again. That began a countdown. A generation in the Bible refers to a group of people living at one time on the planet. God technically has until the last person is left who was alive when Israel was reborn as a nation, to give a time of grace for people to be saved. Therefore, you cannot say things like, "Well, He could come today, or He could come 1,000 years from now; the important thing is that we're ready." No, the generation that sees Israel reborn as a nation will not pass from the earth until all these things are fulfilled. That generation is getting very old. Not only is that generation coming to an end, but it was 2,000 years from Adam to Abraham and 2,000 years from Abraham to Christ. It has almost been 2,000 years since the Church began. We are in the final moments of the last days. The last days didn't begin in the 1980s, they began in 32 AD, and now we are at the final moments of the last days.

> The Lord took hold of me, and I was carried away
> by the Spirit of the Lord to a valley filled with
> bones. He led me all around among the bones
> that covered the valley floor. They were scattered
> everywhere across the ground and were
> completely dried out. Then he asked me, "Son of
> man, can these bones become living people
> again?"

"O Sovereign Lord," I replied, "you alone know the answer to that."

Then he said to me, "Speak a prophetic message to these bones and say, 'Dry bones, listen to the word of the Lord! This is what the Sovereign Lord says: Look! I am going to put breath into you and make you live again! I will put flesh and muscles on you and cover you with skin. I will put breath into you, and you will come to life. Then you will know that I am the Lord.'"

So I spoke this message, just as he told me. Suddenly as I spoke, there was a rattling noise all across the valley, the bones of each body came together and attach themselves as complete skeletons. Then as I watched, muscles and flesh formed over the bones. Then skin formed to cover their bodies, but they still had no breath in them.

Then he said to me, "Speak a prophetic message to the winds, son of man. Speak a prophetic message and say, 'This is what the Sovereign Lord says: Come, O breath, from the four winds! Breathe into these dead bodies so they may live again.'"

So, I spoke the message as he commanded me, and breath came into their bodies. They all came to life and stood up on their feet —a great army.

Then he said to me, "Son of man, these bones represent the people of Israel. They are saying, "We have become old, dry bones —all hope is gone. Our nation is finished.' Therefore, prophesy to them and say, "This is what the Sovereign Lord says: O my people, I will open your graves of exile and cause you to rise again. Then I will bring you back to the land of Israel. When this

> happens, O my people, you will know that I am
> the Lord. I will put my Spirit in you and you will
> live again and return home to your own land.
> Then you will know that I, the Lord, have
> spoken, and I have done what I said. Yes, the
> Lord has spoken!'"

— EZEKIEL 37:1-13

Is this description literal or figurative? It's both. Bible Prophecy has a current manifestation, and it often has a future fulfillment as well. Is it a stretch to say this verse was prophesying the rebirth of the nation of Israel? No, because God said, *"See these bones, they represent the nation of Israel."* Jesus said, *"When you see the fig tree bud again, you'll know."*

Until Israel became a nation, even Bible prophecy scholars did not believe that would ever take place. They said it was impossible. If you look at a map from 1910, there's no Israel, and where it is now was in ruins, occupied by enemies. It seemed like there was no chance of Israel ever becoming a nation. In the 1930s, the Devil raised up Adolf Hitler, a modern-day Hama, whose goal was to make sure prophecy was never fulfilled and to wipe the Jews off the face of Earth. But everything the Devil plans ultimately backfires. Hitler's actions softened people's hearts toward the Jews, and they redrew the borders of the nation of Israel.

ISRAEL, IRAN, RUSSIA AND TURKEY

One of the greatest proofs of Bible prophecy is the rebirth of nations. The book of Ezekiel was written in 592 BC, yet the Bible tells us which nations will be reborn and active. According to scripture, Israel, Iran, Russia, and China will be the major players at the end of time.

> This is another message that came to me from the
> Lord. "Son of man, turn and face Gog of the land
> of Magog, the prince who rules over the nations

> of Meshech and Tubal, and prophesy against
> him. Give this message from the Sovereign
> Lord: Gog, I am your enemy! I will turn you
> around and put hooks in your jaws to lead you
> out with your whole army —your horses and
> charioteers in full armor and a great horde armed
> with shields and swords. Persia, Ethiopia, and
> Libya will join you, too, with all their weapons."

— EZEKIEL 38:1-5

Persia is modern-day Iraq and Iran. Gog and Magog are people groups; you can look up the people alive at that time, then study where they went, where they settled, and which nation they became. Gog and Magog are Russia. Did the Bible nail that prophecy or not? Has Russia been a friend to Israel or an enemy of Israel? If a nation or militant group is being supplied weapons to go against Israel, those weapons typically come from Russia. The Bible tells you the roots of nations and the future of nations. People don't just have a destiny in the Bible, nations also have a prophetic destiny.

According to Ezekiel 38:5, Russia will join Persia, which is Iran and Iraq. Did the Bible nail that or not? Is Iran an enemy of Russia? Do they join together to go against Israel behind the scenes? Nailed it. That's not a small prophecy.

> "Persia, Ethiopia, and Libya will join you, too, with
> all their weapons. Gomer and all its armies will
> also join you, along with the armies of Beth-
> togarmah from the distant north, and many
> others."

— EZEKIEL 38:5-6

Understand that Russia is a massive nation, and many nations mentioned in the Bible are people groups that settled into what is now called Russia.

> "Get ready; be prepared! Keep all the armies around
> you mobilized, and take command of them. A
> long time from now you will be called into
> action. In the distant future you will swoop down
> on the land of Israel, which will be enjoying
> peace after being brought back from the sword or
> recovering from war and after its people have
> returned from many lands to the mountains of
> Israel. You and all your allies —a vast and
> awesome army —will roll down on them like a
> storm and cover the land like a cloud.
>
> "This is what the Sovereign Lord says: At that time
> evil thoughts will come to your mind, and you
> will devise a wicked scheme. You will say,
> 'Israel is an unprotected land filled with
> unwalled villages! I will march against her and
> destroy these people who live in such confi-
> dence! I will go to those formerly desolate cities
> that are now filled with people who have
> returned from exile in many nations. I will
> capture vast amounts of plunder, for the people
> are rich with livestock and other possessions
> now. They think the whole world revolves
> around them!' But Sheba and Dedan and the
> merchants of Tarshish will ask, 'Do you really
> think the armies you have gathered can rob them
> of silver and gold? Do you think you can drive
> away their livestock and seize their goods and
> carry off their plunder?'
>
> "Therefore, son of man, prophesy against Gog. Give
> him this message from the Sovereign Lord:
> When my people are living in peace in their land,

then you will rouse yourself. You will come from your homeland in the distant north…"

— EZEKIEL 38:7-15

Russia sits directly north of Israel; you can know that Putin is taking water routes to attack Israel. He is doing so through the invasion of Ukraine and Crimea. It is all in preparation to attack Israel because Putin needs the Black Sea to get to Israel.

"You will come from your homeland in the distant north and your vast calvary and your mighty army, and you will attack my people Israel, covering their land like a cloud. At that time in the distant future, I will bring you against my land as everyone watches, and my holiness will be displayed by what happens to you, Gog. Then all nations will know that I am the Lord.

"This is what the Sovereign Lord asks: Are you the one I was talking about long ago, when I announced through Israel's prophets that in the future I would bring you against my people? But this is what the Sovereign Lord says: When Gog invades the land of Israel, my fury will boil over! In my jealousy and blazing anger, I promise a mighty shaking in the land of Israel on that day. All living things —the fish in the sea, the birds of the sky, the animals of the field, the small animals that scurry along the ground, and the people of the earth —will quake in terror at my presence. Mountains will be thrown down; cliffs will crumble; walls will fall to the earth. I will summon the sword against you on all the hills of Israel, says the Sovereign Lord. Your men will turn their swords against each other. I will punish

you and your armies with disease and bloodshed;
I will send torrential rain, hailstones, fire, and
burning sulfur! In this way, I will show my great-
ness and holiness, and I will make myself known
to all the nations of the world. Then they will
know that I am the Lord."

— EZEKIEL 38:15-23

How can you have a brain and not live for God now? This book is not
guesswork. Bible prophecy is history written before it takes place.

"Son of man, prophesy against Gog. Give him this
message from the Sovereign Lord: I am your
enemy, O Gog, ruler of the nations of Meshech
and Tubal. I will turn you around and drive you
toward the mountains of Israel, bringing you
from the distant north."

— EZEKIEL 39:1-2

"Persia, Ethiopia, and Libya will join you, too, with
all their weapons. Gomer and all its armies will
also join you, along with the armies of Beth-
togarmah, from the distant north, and many
others."

— EZEKIEL 38:5-6

The Bible prophesied that Russia (Gog and Magog), Turkey, Iran, and
Beth-togarmah will gather. Why is Russia moving into Crimea and Ukraine
right now? The Bible says those actions precipitate the attack on Israel.
We're basically living in Ezekiel 38:5-6 right now. Right now, Russia is
retaking the nations it needs to get a straight path to Israel. In the '80s,
Lester Sumrall said, "People are saying that Gorbachev is going to attack

Israel, but it can't happen now because, according to the Bible, they have to take Crimea back." Russia got Crimea back in 2014. If Russia has the backing of China, is it going to make a difference if Europe and America oppose them?

If you don't know Bible prophecy, you're just a fool. You'll be an easily deceived fool because you'll see Muslim immigration as compassion for people. You won't see that there are nations actively working to take Israel off the face of the Earth; they seek to destroy Israel by weakening Israel's allies.

> "Son of man prophesy against Gog. Give him this
>   message from the Sovereign Lord: I am your
>   enemy, O Gog, ruler of the nations of Meshach
>   and Tubal. I will turn you around and drive you
>   toward the mountains of Israel, bringing you
>   from the distant north. I will knock the bow from
>   your left hand and the arrows from your right
>   hand, and I will leave you helpless. You and your
>   army and your allies will all die on the moun-
>   tains. I will feed you to the vultures and wild
>   animals. You will fall in the open fields, for I
>   have spoken, says the Sovereign Lord. And I
>   will rain down fire on Magog and on all your
>   allies who lives safely on the coasts. Then they
>   will know that I am the Lord.
> "In this way I will make known my holy name
>   among the people of Israel. I will not let anyone
>   bring shame on it. And the nations, too, will
>   know that I am the Lord, the Holy One of Israel.
>   That day of judgment will come, says the
>   Sovereign Lord. Everything will happen just as I
>   have declared it.
> "Then the people of the towns of Israel will go out
>   and pick up your small and large shields, bows

and arrows, javelins and spears, and they will use
them for fuel. There will be enough to last them
seven years! They won't need to cut wood from
the fields or forests, for these weapons will give
them all the fuel they need. They will plunder
those who planned to plunder them, and they
will rob those who planned to rob them, says the
Sovereign Lord.

"And I will make a vast graveyard for Gog and his
hordes in the Valley of the Travelers, east of the
Dead Sea. It will block the way of those who
traveled there, and they will change the name of
the place to the Valley of Gog's Hordes. It will
take seven months for the people of Israel to
bury the bodies and cleanse the land. Everyone
in Israel will help, for it will be a glorious
victory for Israel when I demonstrate my glory
on that day, says the Sovereign Lord.

"After seven months, teams of men will be
appointed to search the land for skeletons to
bury, so the land can be made clean again.
Whenever bones are found, a marker will be set
up so that burial crews will take them to be
buried in the Valley of Gog's Hordes. (There will
be a town there named Hamonah, which means
'horde.') And so the land will finally be
cleansed.

"And now, son of man, this is what the Sovereign
Lord says: Call all the birds and wild animals.
Say to them: Gather together for my great sacrificial feast. Come from far and near to the mountains of Israel, and there eat flesh and drink
blood! Eat the flesh of mighty men and drink the
blood of princes as though they were rams,
lambs, goats and bulls —all fattened animals

from Bashan! Gorge yourselves with flesh until you are glutted; drink blood until you are drunk. This is the sacrificial feast I have prepared for you. Feast at my banquet table —feast on horses and charioteers, on mighty men and all kinds of valiant warriors, says the Sovereign Lord.

"In this way, I will demonstrate my glory to the nations. Everyone will see the punishment I have inflicted on them and the power of my fist when I strike. And from that time on the people of Israel will know that I am the LORD their God. The nations will know why Israel was sent away to exile —it was punishment for sin, for they were unfaithful to their God. Therefore, I turned away from them and let their enemies destroy them. I turned my face away and punished them because of their defilement and their sins.

"So now this is what the Sovereign Lord says: I will end the captivity of my people; I will have mercy on all Israel, for I jealously guard my holy reputation! They will accept responsibility for their past shame, and unfaithfulness after they come home to live in peace in their own land, with no one to bother them. When I bring them home from the lands of their enemies, I will display my holiness among them for all the nations to see. Then my people will know that I am the LORD their God, because I sent them away to exile and brought them home again. I will leave none of my people behind. And I will never again turn my face from them, for I will pour out my Spirit upon the people of Israel. I, the Sovereign Lord, have spoken."

— EZEKIEL 39:1-29

There you have the destiny of Israel, Russia, Iran, and Turkey. Israel has never had a revival in the Church age, but it will have a revival.

CHINA

> Then the sixth angel blew his trumpet, and I heard a voice speaking from the four horns of the gold altar that stands in the presence of God. And the voice said to the sixth angel who held the trumpet, "Release the four angels who are bound at the great Euphrates River." Then the four angels who had been prepared for this hour and day and month and year were turned loose to kill one-third of all the people on the earth. I heard the size of their army, which was 200 million mounted troops.
>
> — REVELATION 9:13-16

People have used this scripture to mock Bible prophecy; they would question how there could ever be an army of 200 million people. When John wrote this, there were 300 million people on Earth. Meaning, for you to have an army of 200 million people at that time, you would have had to get two-thirds of the world assembled as an army. That would have been impossible, especially if you take the number of elderly people and children into account.

> Then the sixth angel poured out his bowl on the great Euphrates River, and it dried up so that the kings from the east could march their armies towards the west without hindrance.
>
> — REVELATION 16:12

How is this army going to move from the east? Remember, whenever the Bible speaks about direction, it's always from Jerusalem, not Detroit. So, when it says that this 200-million-man army will move from the east to Israel, you know that they will march from China because China sits east of Israel. Just like you can track Gog and Magog, you can track the kings of the east and see they are actually China. They're going to march through the dried-up Euphrates River as a road. People used to say that could never happen because the Euphrates River is one of the oldest rivers. Yet, in 2009 the New York Times published an article titled "Iraq Suffers as the Euphrates River Dwindles."[1] The New York Times even mentioned in this article that the book of Revelation prophesied its drying up as a sign of the end times. These are not shot-in-the-dark prophecies; these are not Nostradamus vague references. The Bible says the Euphrates River will dry up, and a 200-million-man army will march on its dry riverbed to attack Israel. People thought it was impossible for the Euphrates River to dry up, yet it already has. People thought there couldn't be a 200-million-man army, and now there is a nation that can produce such an army.

The other thing people used to mock in the Bible was that the soldiers would ride on horses. Yet, when they were looking for Osama bin Laden— or pretending to—they discovered that traveling by horse works better in the Middle East than traveling by tanks or Humvees. Tanks got stuck, vehicles got stuck, horses didn't get stuck. Tanks have trouble in the mountain; horses have no trouble there.

AMERICA

In the '80s, Lester Sumrall said that a time will come when America abandons Israel because the Bible says she'll be left by herself. That seemed impossible in the '80s. If you were a politician and you wanted to go against Israel, Democrat or Republican, you were out. Nobody held that view. Yet, now you hear American politicians routinely sound-off against Israel. You had the governor of New York City threatening to close all of the synagogues. That same spirit that was in Haman is now in many politicians. It was once popular to support Israel, now it's popular to go against

Israel. In fact, we now have a Secretary of State who's friendly with Iran, a country actively building up nuclear warheads to wipe Israel off the face of the earth. It all aligns with Bible prophecy.

This isn't the 1980s. Our military used to know how to fight; now, they know how to use correct gender pronouns. America's military is turning into an army of transgender, easily-killed military members while these other nations grow in strength. This seemed impossible when I was a kid, but no one fears America anymore.

America is not mentioned in Bible prophecy. Israel is not going to have any allies. The move by current American politicians to abandon Israel is another sign that you're in the final moments of the last days, and it's going to culminate in a war in the Valley of Meggido.

ARMAGEDDON

> They deliberately forget that God made the heavens
>   long ago by the word of his command, and he
>   brought the earth out from the water and
>   surrounded it with water. Then he used the water
>   to destroy the ancient world with a mighty
>   flood. And by the same word, the present
>   heavens and earth have been stored up for fire.
>   They are being kept for the day of judgment,
>   when ungodly people will be destroyed.
> But you must not forget this one thing, dear friends:
>   A day is like a thousand years to the Lord, and a
>   thousand years is like a day. The Lord isn't really
>   being slow about his promise, as some people
>   think. No, he is being patient for your sake. He
>   does not want anyone to be destroyed, but wants
>   everyone to repent. But the day of the Lord will
>   come as unexpectedly as a thief. Then the
>   heavens will pass away with a terrible noise, and

> the very elements themselves will disappear in
> fire, and the earth and everything on it will be
> found to deserve judgment.
> Since everything around us is going to be destroyed
> like this, what holy and godly lives you should
> live, looking forward to the day of God and
> hurrying it along. On that day, he will set the
> heavens on fire, and the elements will melt away
> in the flames.
>
> — 2 PETER 3:5-12

What kind of intense heat that burns in the heavens could this be talking about?

> And the Lord will send the plague on all the nations
> that fought against Jerusalem. Their people will
> become like walking corpses, their flesh rotting
> away. Their eyes will melt in their sockets, and
> their tongues will melt in their mouths.
>
> — ZECHARIAH 14:12

> The same plague will strike the horses, mules,
> camels, donkeys, and all the other animals in the
> enemy camps.
>
> — ZECHARIAH 14:15

In Ezekiel's time, a fire had to be lit or shot with an arrow, so how could a fire engulf the heavens and expose everything on the earth to judgment?

Thousands of nuclear warheads are not stockpiled without a reason. They will be launched at a battle in the valley of Megiddo, which the Bible calls Armageddon. All the nations of the world will unite to make war against

Israel, and the Antichrist will lead them. China, Russia, Turkey, Syria, Iran, and Ethiopia will lead the swarm on Israel like a horde. Then Christ will return and deliver Israel at the Second Coming.

WHAT CAN YOU DO ABOUT IT?

If you don't know what to do, you'll be paralyzed; you won't get married, you won't have children, you won't start a business. 2 Peter 3:11-12 says, *"Since everything around us is going to be destroyed like this, what holy and godly lives you should live, looking forward to the day of God and hurrying it along."*

If there's a stream that's controlled by the Devil—and there is—then you need to get in the opposite flow that's controlled by God. In God's stream, you will prosper when others are in financial turmoil, you will enjoy healing and protection when others are sick and dying, you will be blessed when others are cursed. That goes for you and your family. In this hour, you can still say, "As for me and my house, we will serve the Lord." If this stirred up your spirit, you know there's a God-part on the inside of you. *"Deep calleth unto deep."* On the inside of you is a spirit that longs for communion with God, and God communes with us through His Word.

8

THE RAPTURE OF THE CHURCH

INTRODUCTION TO THE RAPTURE

The book of Revelations' full name is The Revelation of Jesus Christ; the book's purpose is to point you to Jesus. It does not point you to powdered milk, AK47s, an ammunition supply, or an underground bunker. It points you to Christ. When talking about end-time Bible prophecy, everyone's mind generally gravitates to the Rapture. People have many questions about the Rapture, but by the end of this chapter, you won't have any questions. Now, if you stay focused on what I'm saying and not get into what I'm not saying, it will be more profitable.

> Then, together with them, we who are still alive and
> remain on the earth will be caught up in the
> clouds to meet the Lord in the air. Then we will
> be with the Lord forever. So encourage and
> comfort each other with these words.
>
> — 1 THESSALONIANS 4:17-18

Concerning end-time Bible prophecy, the Bible says to encourage and comfort each other with these words. If anyone teaches prophecy in a way that makes you afraid and uneasy as a Christian, something is off with the teaching. Now, if you're not right with God, that teaching should literally scare the hell out of you. The Bible says some are saved by fear; it shouldn't be comforting if you're not a Christian.

> Night is the time when people sleep and drinkers get
>> drunk. But let us who live in the light be clear-
>> headed, protected by the armor of faith and love,
>> and wearing as our helmet the confidence of our
>> salvation.
> For God chose to save us through our Lord Jesus
>> Christ, not to pour out his anger on us.
>
> — 1 THESSALONIANS 5:7-9

The Tribulation is God pouring out His wrath on the earth. But God chooses not to pour out His anger upon us, the Church. In The Dake Annotated Reference Bible, Finis Dake notes, "God has not appointed Christians to go through the Tribulation wrath, or the sudden destruction of verses two to three, or the wrath of eternal hell, but to be delivered by rapture so that whether we live or die, we should live together with Him forever."

Christ died for us; whether we are dead or alive when He returns, we can live with Him forever. So, encourage each other, and build each other up. Again, if you hear the teaching on the Rapture and it makes you have to go on mind medication for panic attacks, it's probably not the way Paul taught it. I'm not nervous, I'm not unhappy, I'm at peace. *"Since everything around us is going to be destroyed like this, what holy and godly lives you should live."* (2 Peter 3:11 NLT)

Kenneth Hagin wrote in his book, *The Triumphant Church*, that there are 3 types of beliefs regarding the Church. The first is the defeated Church, where they believe the Devil's out there attacking us, and we just need to hold on until the end. Post-Tribulation Rapture people fall into this category because you can't simultaneously believe the Church has dominion over the Devil and believe the Devil will take dominion over the Church in the Tribulation.

Kenneth Hagin describes the second group as the warring Church; most Christians fall into this group. You'll hear them say things like, "We're going to have a crusade, but that region's full of witches and demons. We just really need to pray." The Devil is under our feet, whether you pray or not. You don't pray to hope the Devil stays under your feet; Christ already stripped him of his power.

Then you have the third group described by Kenneth Hagin, the victorious Church. This group says things like, "We're not trying to get victory over the Devil. We have victory over the Devil and all his power because of what Jesus did 2,000 years ago." The Devil's out there waiting to attack, but he can stay out there waiting because he is under your feet, and you can't get attacked by something under your feet.

> Look, I have given you authority over all the power
> of the enemy, and you can walk among snakes
> and scorpions and crush them. Nothing will
> injure you.
>
> — LUKE 10:19

> Now, dear brothers and sisters, let us clarify some
> things about the coming of the Lord Jesus Christ
> and how we will be gathered to meet him. Don't
> be so easily shaken or alarmed by those who say
> the day of the Lord has already begun. Don't
> believe them, even if they claim to have a spiri-
> tual vision, a revelation, or a letter from us.
> Don't be fooled by what they say. For that day
> will not come until there is a great rebellion
> against God and the man of lawlessness is
> revealed—the one who brings destruction. He

will exalt himself and defy everything that
people call god and every object of worship. He
will even sit in the temple of God, claiming that
he himself is God.

Don't you remember that I told you about this when
I was with you? And you know what is holding
him back, for he can only be revealed when his
time comes. For this lawlessness is already at
work secretly, and it will remain secret until the
one who is holding it back steps out of the way.
Then the man of lawlessness will be revealed,
but the Lord Jesus will slay him with the breath
of his mouth and destroy him by the splendor of
his coming.

This man will come to do the work of Satan with
counterfeit power and signs and miracles. He
will use every kind of evil deception to fool
those who are on their way to destruction,
because they refuse to love and accept the truth
that would save them. So God will cause them to
be greatly deceived, and they will believe all
these lies. Then they will be condemned for
enjoying evil rather than believing the truth.

— 2 THESSALONIANS 2:1-12

Then, leaving the crowds outside, Jesus went into
the house. His disciples said, "Please explain to
us the the story of the weeds in the field."

Jesus replied, "The Son of Man is the farmer who
plants the good seed. The field is the world and
the good seed represents the people of the Kingdom. The weeds are the people who belong to
the evil one. The enemy who planted the weeds
among the wheat is the devil. The harvest is the

end of the world, and the harvesters are the
angels.

"Just as the weeds are sorted out and burned in the
fire, so it will be at the end of the world. The Son
of Man will send his angels, and they will
remove from his Kingdom everything that
causes sin and all who do evil. And the angels
will throw them into the fiery furnace, where
there will be weeping and gnashing of teeth.
Then the righteous will shine like the sun in their
Father's Kingdom. Anyone with ears to hear
should listen and understand!"

— MATTHEW 13:36-43

"The Kingdom of Heaven is like a farmer who
planted good seed in his field. But that night as
the workers slept, his enemy came and planted
weeds among the wheat, then slipped away.
When the crop began to grow and produce grain,
the weeds also grew.

"The farmer's workers went to him and said, 'Sir,
the field where you planted that good seed is full
of weeds! Where did they come from?'

"'An enemy has done this!' the farmer exclaimed.

"'Should we uproot the weeds?' they asked.

"'No,' he replied, 'you'll uproot the wheat if you
do.'"

— MATTHEW 13:24-29

God will not start judging the wicked people in the world until there is a
way to do so without damaging the righteous people in the world. Just as
Jesus said in the parable, to not uproot the tares because doing so would
damage the wheat. Any time there's a tragedy, you always hear some

dummy who's a Christian leader say, "I believe God sent Hurricane Katrina. I believe God did that because New Orleans was scheduled to have a gay pride parade that week, and God judged the city." No, this parable tells you how God thinks. Even if wicked military people find out there's a terrorist cell meeting in a specific place, if there are children nearby, they won't strike it, let alone if their own children are there. Similarly, God said He won't judge the place if His children are there. Then what do we do?

> Let both grow together until the harvest: and in the
> time of harvest I will say to the reapers, Gather
> ye together first the tares, and bind them in
> bundles to burn them: but gather the wheat into
> my barn.
>
> — MATTHEW 13:30 (KJV)

Before any military invades, they call their ambassadors home first. In the same way, the Rapture is the calling home of God's ambassadors to the earth. While we're on Earth, we're warning the people of the world, then when the time of grace is over, we're called home.

THE SEVEN RAPTURES IN THE BIBLE

In your human mind, it's difficult to believe there will be a rapture, but seeing that the Rapture is not a new concept in the Bible will really help your faith. In using the word "rapture" here, I mean instances where someone is taken up out of the earth into Heaven in their mortal body. There are seven raptures in the Bible.

Number one: Enoch.

> Enoch lived 365 years, walking in close fellowship
> with God. Then one day he disappeared, because
> God took him.
>
> — GENESIS 5:23-24

He was walking with God closely, and he never died. He was taken up into Heaven.

Number two: Elijah.

> As they were walking along and talking, suddenly a
> chariot of fire appeared, drawn by horses of fire.
> It drove between the two men, separating them,
> and Elijah was carried by a whirlwind into
> heaven.
>
> — 2 KINGS 2:11

Elijah didn't go up in a chariot of fire; a chariot of fire went by him, and Elijah went up in a whirlwind. He was still alive.

Number three: Moses.

> Then Moses climbed the mountain to appear before
> God. The Lord called to him from the mountain
> and said, "Give these instructions to the family
> of Jacob; announce it to the descendants of
> Israel."
>
> — EXODUS 19:3

> The Lord came down on the top of Mount Sinai and
> called Moses to the top of the mountain. So
> Moses climbed the mountain.
>
> — EXODUS 19:20

This one's the most arguable of the seven raptures in the Bible, but Moses was called up to appear before God. In his mortal body, Moses appeared before God the Father on top of a mountain, in a cloud.

Number four: Jesus.

> After saying this, Jesus was taken up into a cloud
> while they were watching, and they could no
> longer see him. As they strained to see him
> rising into heaven, two white-robed men
> suddenly stood among them. "Men of Galilee,"
> they said, "why are you standing here staring
> into heaven? Jesus has been taken from you into
> heaven, but someday he will return from heaven
> in the same way you saw him go!"
>
> — ACTS 1:9-11

Number five: Paul.

> I was caught up to the third heaven fourteen years
> ago. Whether I was in my body or out of my
> body, I don't know—only God knows. Yes, only
> God knows whether I was in my body or outside
> my body. But I do know that I was caught up to
> paradise and heard things so astounding that they
> cannot be expressed in words, things no human
> is allowed to tell.
>
> — 2 CORINTHIANS 12:2-4

The following raptures are in the future:

Number six: The Church.

> For God chose to save us through our Lord Jesus
> Christ, not to pour out his anger on us. Christ
> died for us so that, whether we are dead or alive
> when he returns, we can live with him forever.
> So, encourage each other and build each other
> up, just as you are already doing.
>
> — 1 THESSALONIANS 5:9-11

Number seven: The two prophets.

> But after three and a half days, God breathed life
> into them, and they stood up! Terror struck all
> who were staring at them. Then a loud voice
> from heaven called to the two prophets, "Come
> up here!" And they rose to heaven in a cloud as
> their enemies watched.
>
> — REVELATION 11:11-12

If you feel like the Rapture is a far-out concept, there it is, all throughout
the Bible; people in their mortal bodies being caught up off the earth into a
cloud to meet with God.

IMPORTANCE OF A PRE-TRIBULATION RAPTURE

I've never met anyone who believed in a post-Tribulation Rapture or a
mid-Tribulation Rapture that wasn't a defeatist—a depressed type of
person. It's important to understand the pre-Tribulation Rapture, or else it
will bleed into your theology on healing and victory. 1 Thessalonians 4:13
tells us that the Rapture is Christ coming back in the clouds for the Church.

The word rapture appears nowhere in the Bible because the Bible wasn't written in English. The word in Greek that refers to the catching up of the saints is *harpazō*, which was then translated into the Latin word *raptis*, where we get "rapture".

The second coming is after the Rapture when Christ returns with the saints and touches down on the earth.

> For the Lord himself will come down from heaven
>> with a commanding shout, with the voice of the
>> archangel, and with the trumpet call of God.
> First, the believers who have died will rise from
>> their graves. Then, together with them, we who
>> are still alive and remain on the earth will be
>> caught up in the clouds to meet the Lord in
> the air.

> — 1 THESSALONIANS 4:16-17

You will hear some people say, "I feel like we're going through the Tribulation right now. I mean, there's all kinds of crazy stuff happening." The Bible talks about birth pains before the Rapture, that the earth will be in a difficult place before the Rapture, but the problems you're seeing now are caused by sin. The Bible says the wages of sin are what? Death. Sin brings a curse without any help from God. If there's a rebellion against God, sin comes in, and sin is a magnet for the curse. That's not God's judgment, that's sin doing its thing. However, after the Rapture, judgment is poured out from Heaven, and that's a whole new ballgame. The Bible says right now is the time of God's wonderful favor, no longer counting people's sins against them. When we claim a pre-Tribulation Rapture, we're not saying the Church will never have obstacles; the church has always had obstacles. We're talking about tribulation wrath that comes from Heaven.

10 PROOFS OF A PRE-TRIBULATION RAPTURE

The first and most important proof of a pre-Tribulation Rapture is the dominion of the Church. This is indisputable. If greater is He who lives in you than he who lives in the world, how would the Antichrist ever exercise dominion over the church and take over the world?

The Church is noted in 2 Thessalonians 2:6-7 as the "restrainer." What we have in us keeps the Antichrist from being revealed and doing what he wants. God does not run on Satan's clock; Satan runs on God's clock. When you read history, you see that Satan has always had to have an Antichrist ready because he doesn't know when the Rapture will be. Hitler tried to carry it out, but he couldn't do it because there was a Church in the earth that has power over the Devil. Adam was given full dominion over the earth, and Adam sinned against God. The Bible says in Romans 6:16 that whoever you obey becomes your master. Therefore, Satan had the dominion transferred from Adam to himself when Adam sinned; that's why Satan is referred to in 2 Corinthians 4:4 as the God of this world.

When Jesus was in the wilderness, Satan told him…

> "I will give you the glory of these kingdoms and
> authority over them," the devil said, "because
> they are mine to give to anyone I please. I will
> give it all to you if you will worship me."
>
> — LUKE 4:6-7

When Satan said this to Jesus, Jesus never challenged the statement because it was true. But when Jesus died as the second Adam, the Bible says he took the keys of dominion from Satan. That's why he said to John, *"behold, I have the keys of death, hell, and the grave."* Jesus gave that authority to the Church.

Ephesians 1 and 2 says we have been raised together with Him and are seated far above all principalities and powers. The Devil has been put under our feet.

Though Antichrist will be possessed by Satan himself, Satan is defeated and under the church's feet. With all of these things being irrevocably true, how would the Antichrist then, through demonic power, take dominion back from the Church? If the Antichrist usurps authority over the Church, he would have to ascend above Christ—if you accept that doctrinal reasoning, you're on a bad road. There is no way for the Antichrist to do what he is going to do while the body of Christ is on the earth. One Christian full of the Holy Ghost would be able to get on a plane and go to wherever the Antichrist is, and cast the Devil out of him. Anyone that doesn't understand the pre-Tribulation Rapture also does not understand the dominion of the Church; you cannot justify the two things.

The second proof of a pre-Tribulation Rapture is that the book of Revelation mentions the Church 19 times through chapters 1-3. After John is called up out of the earth in the spirit (Revelation 4:2), there is no further mention of the Church. Then you read that the wrath of God begins to be poured out on the earth.

> The Revelation of Jesus Christ, which God gave
> unto him, to shew unto his servants things which
> must shortly come to pass; and he sent and signi-
> fied it by his angel unto the servant John.

> — REVELATION 1:1 (KJV)

Jesus appears to John, listen to what He says:

> Write the things which thou hast seen, and the things
> which are, and the things which shall be
> hereafter.

> — REVELATION 1:19 (KJV)

Revelation 2:1 says, *"Write unto the angel of the church of Ephesus,"* which any Bible scholar will tell you that the angel of the church is the pastor of the church. Notice how he wrote to the pastor, not the board. It finishes in Revelation 3:22. *"He that hath an ear, let him hear what the spirit sayeth unto the churches."*

> After this I looked, and, behold, a door was opened
> in heaven: and the first voice which I heard was
> as it were of a trumpet talking with me; which
> said, Come up hither, and I will shew thee things
> which must be hereafter.
> And immediately I was in the spirit: and, behold, a
> throne was set in heaven, and one sat on the
> throne.
>
> — REVELATION 4:1-2 (KJV)

The third proof of a pre-Tribulation Rapture is where Jesus tells us what the earth is like when the Rapture happens.

> "When the Son of Man returns, it will be like it was
> in Noah's day. In those days before the flood, the
> people were enjoying banquets and parties and
> weddings right up to the time Noah entered his
> boat. People didn't realize what was going to
> happen until the flood came and swept them all
> away. That is the way it will be when the Son of
> Man comes."
>
> — MATTHEW 24:37-39

God decided to judge the earth because of the stench of sin, but not one drop of rain fell until the righteous were sealed in the ark. God has never poured out His judgment on the earth while His people were still present. There wasn't a heavy rain, then Noah grabbed a log and swam to the ark; Noah wasn't treading water for 40 days and 40 nights. Noah was inside eating and drinking on a cruise ship. And as it was in the days of Noah, so it will be in the day when the Son of Man appears.

The fourth proof of a pre-Tribulation Rapture is found in the story of Lot. As it was in the days of Lot, so it'll be in the day when the Son of Man returns. As Lot and his family delayed, angels hurried them out of the city. And when they were clear, fire and brimstone rained down from Heaven on Sodom and Gomorrah. Was Lot ducking and diving fire and brimstone and barely able to run out of the city? No. No fire or brimstone fell until angels took them out of the city.

The parallels are striking, are they not? Angels will harvest the wheat, angels sealed Noah in the boat, angels hurried Lot's family out of the city, and then the judgment fell.

The fifth proof is that the Bible says that as children of God, we are kept from the hour of great testing that comes upon those who belong to this world. The Bible says, "You have not received the spirit of this world, but you've received the Spirit of Christ." This should not be difficult for you to understand.

> Because thou hast kept the word of my patience, I
> also will keep thee from the hour of temptation,
> which shall come upon all the world, to try them
> that dwell upon the earth.
>
> — REVELATION 3:10 (KJV)

The New Living Translation puts it like this, "*Because you have obeyed my command to persevere, I will protect you from the great time of testing that will come upon the whole world to test those who belong to the world.*"

There are striking parts of that passage; God says He'll protect us from judgment and that it is not for the church but rather for those who belong to the world. Like Noah and Lot, the Tribulation is not a judgment for everybody; the righteous are never judged with the wicked.

> I am coming soon. Hold on to what you have, so that
> no one will take away your crown.

> — REVELATION 3:11

You can lose what God gives you, but you don't have to.

> "All who are victorious will become pillars in the
> Temple of my God, and they will never have to
> leave it. And I will write on them the name of
> my God, and they will be citizens in the city of
> my God —the new Jerusalem that comes down
> from heaven from my God. And I will also write
> on them my new name."

> — REVELATION 3:12

Heaven is the home of overcomers.

Our sixth proof is based on the parable of the wheat and the tares found in Matthew 13.

> "...'Should we pull out the weeds?' they asked.
> "'No,' he replied, 'you'll uproot the wheat if you do.
> Let both grow together until the harvest. Then I
> will tell the harvesters to sort out the weeds...'"

> — MATTHEW 13:28-30

In this parable, the servants wanted to pull up the tares, but Jesus said not to because it would harm the wheat as well. Jesus said the angels will gather and sort both the wheat and the tares at the harvest time, alluding to the Rapture of the Church.

The seventh proof of a pre-Tribulation Rapture is found in 2 Thessalonians 2:6-7. It says:

> And you know what is holding him back, for he can
>   be revealed only when his time comes. For this
>   lawlessness is already at work secretly, and it
>   will remain secret until the one who is holding it
>   back steps out of the way.
>
> — 2 THESSALONIANS 2:6-7

The restrainer must be removed before the Antichrist goes public. The Church will continue to hinder lawlessness until the Rapture, and then the Antichrist will be revealed.

The eighth proof is that there is no mention of a resurrection of the dead during the Second Coming. So, if you're a post-Tribulation person, where is the mention of the dead in Christ rising at the Second Coming? There has to be an event that precedes it because Christ returns with the saints. It does not say that He returns and they come up alive again.

The ninth proof is found in 1 Thessalonians 5:9-11, a promise assuring us that saints will escape the wrath of God.

> For God hath not appointed us to wrath, but to
>   obtain salvation by our Lord Jesus Christ,
> Who died for us, that, whether we wake or sleep, we
>   should live together with him.
> Wherefore comfort yourselves together, and edify
>   one another, even as also ye do.
>
> — I THESSALONIANS 5:9-11 (KJV)

How could saints comfort one another, as stated in this scripture, if the only hope they had was the coming wrath of God and future tribulation? Without a pre-Tribulation Rapture, we would not want to focus on end-time Bible prophecy; there would be no words of comfort or encouragement. But the Bible says that these words are a comfort and an encouragement. We know we are not sticking around for the Tribulation; we don't have to stock up on food and ammunition or build a bomb shelter.

Jesus said:

> Watch ye therefore, and pray always, that ye may be
> accounted worthy to escape all these things that
> shall come to pass, and to stand before the Son
> of man.
>
> — LUKE 21:36 (KJV)

The tenth proof of a pre-Tribulation Rapture is the change of God's attitude towards humanity and the Church is never mentioned after Revelation 4:1. In Revelation chapters 1-3, God says, in effect, "Warn them, make sure they're okay. I'm going to strengthen you so that you can make it." Then starting in chapter four, God says, in effect, "I'm done with you. Now you're going to pay," because His children are no longer on the earth at this point.

Don't confuse the Church with the Tribulation saints. There are people saved after the Rapture, but it's not us (The Church), we're saved now. The Bible says these things are written so that you may know that you have life eternal. You can know you're saved. If you can't confidently say you are saved, God didn't attract you to this book to receive information about Bible prophecy, He wants you to be ready for the coming of the Lord. If you've never received Jesus Christ, you must be born again. If you think 2020 was bad, the Bible says that this is the beginning of the horrors to come.

If you need to be born again, I want you to say this out loud, from your heart:

> "Heavenly Father, I admit that I've sinned. I repent. I believe in my heart you raised Jesus from the dead. I confess with my mouth that Jesus is my Lord and Savior. Right now, I receive forgiveness. By the blood of Jesus, I am saved. I am forgiven. I am clean. In Jesus' name. Amen."

9

PROPHETIC SIGNS AND THE FULFILLMENT OF BIBLE PROPHECY

SIGNS

I'm torn over how deep to go into the "climate emergency" because it dates the book. If you're reading this way in the future, we had this thing called COVID-19. It swept through the earth and allowed government leaders to see how far they could push people and test totalitarian control. Now it appears the plan is to shift from COVID-19 to a climate emergency. Soon we will need to do all the same things we're doing for COVID-19 to stop rapid climate change; let's talk about this and other happenings in the light of Bible prophecy.

> Later, Jesus sat on the Mount of Olives. His disciples came to him privately and said, "Tell us, when will all this happen? What sign will signal your return and the end of the world?"
> Jesus told them, "Don't let anyone mislead you, for many will come in my name claiming, 'I am the Messiah.' They will deceive many. And you will hear of wars and threats of wars, but don't panic.

> Yes, these things must take place, but the end
> won't follow immediately. Nation will go to war
> against nation, and kingdom against kingdom.
> There will be famines..."
>
> — MATTHEW 24:3-7

What are the specific signs Christ mentioned as a mark of his return being near? Famines, drought, and rivers drying up that never had before. Earthquakes in diverse places, meaning there will be severe earthquakes where there's never been any. New incurable sickness and disease. Strange tides and roaring seas; tsunamis. They'll say it's wrong to eat meat and it's wrong to marry or be given away in marriage. There will be signs in the heavens.

Will these events cause people to repent or say we must save the planet? The signs Jesus mentions are intended to cause people to repent when they realize this present Earth will pass away. Arrogant people will see these prophetic signs happen but won't turn to God. Let's look at the signs in more detail.

PLAGUES AND FAMINE

> Some of his disciples began talking about the
> majestic stonework of the Temple and the
> memorial decorations on the walls. But Jesus
> said, "The time is coming when all these things
> will be completely demolished. Not one stone
> will be left on top of another!"
> "Teacher," they asked, "when will all this happen?
> What sign will show us that these things are
> about to take place?"
> He replied, "Don't let anyone mislead you, for
> many will come in my name, claiming, 'I am
> the Messiah,' and saying, 'The time has come!'

But don't believe them. And when you hear of
wars and insurrections, don't panic. Yes, these
things must take place first, but the end won't
follow immediately." Then he added, "Nation
will go to war against nation, and kingdom
against kingdom. There will be great earthquakes, and there will be famines and plagues in
many lands..."

— LUKE 21:5-11

Notice it is famines and plagues *plural*. He didn't say there'll be *a* plague,
He said there'll be plagues, and they'll be like a woman's birth pains; they
will get worse and more frequent with time. So, if you shut your church
down for COVID-19, you're going to be shutting your church down a lot
in the future.

EARTHQUAKES

Jesus said there will be famines and earthquakes in many lands, meaning
there will be earthquakes where there've never been before. For example,
an earthquake in a diverse place is like when you hear of an earthquake in a
place like Indiana, and there's no record of an earthquake ever in Indiana.
These will be the first birth pains, with more to come.

My wife gave birth to our daughter Camila, so I know a little bit about
childbirth—very little. When women start getting birth pains, they don't
get farther apart and weaker; they get stronger and closer together until the
baby is born. One criticism people have of Bible prophecy is that Jesus said
there are going to be earthquakes, but there have always been earthquakes.
These critics don't understand that Jesus is saying they will be like a
woman's birth pains; they'll become more severe and closer together
before the coming of the Lord. I've heard people say on the news that there
used to be one tsunami every 500 years, and now we've had 3 in the last 10
years. Jesus said to not be afraid when you see these things coming more

frequently, but to...*take heart, for your redemption draws nigh (Luke 21:28).*

> Immediately after the anguish of those days, the sun
> will be darkened, the moon will give no light, the
> stars will fall from the sky, and the powers in the
> heavens will be shaken.
>
> — MATTHEW 24:29

TSUNAMIS

> "And there will be strange signs in the sun, moon,
> and stars. And here on earth the nations will be
> in turmoil, perplexed by the roaring seas and
> strange tides."
>
> — LUKE 21:25

There will be strange signs in the sun, the moon, and the stars. And here on Earth, the nations will be in turmoil, perplexed by the roaring seas and strange tides—tsunamis. The Bible says this is a sign that Christ is coming soon, but what will the earth do when they see that happen? They'll say, "Man, the oceans had this same tide since recorded history; now it's flowing in the other direction. We need to stop using plastic." But the Bible says this present Earth will end; you can use all the paper straws you want, but you're not going to reverse any of this.

FORBIDDING THE EATING OF MEAT

> The next day as Cornelius's messengers were
> nearing the town, Peter went up on the flat roof
> to pray. It was about noon, and he was hungry.
> But while the meal was being prepared, he fell

into a trance. He saw the sky open, and something like a large sheet was let down by its four
corners. In the sheet were all sorts of animals,
reptiles, and birds. Then a voice said to him,
"Get up, Peter; kill and eat them."
"No Lord," Peter declared. "I've never eaten
anything that our Jewish laws have declared
impure and unclean."
But the voice spoke again: "Do not call something
unclean If God has made it clean." The same
vision was repeated three times. Then the sheet
was suddenly pulled up to heaven.

— ACTS 10:9-16

They'll say it's wrong to eat meat and other foods, but God created those foods to be eaten with thanks by faithful people who know the truth. Everything God created is good; this doesn't say all food is good. So, if you look at the ingredients and see words you can't pronounce, it's not food created by God. We should not reject any food created by God, but receive it with thanksgiving, for it is made holy and acceptable by the Word of God and prayer, and that's one of the reasons we pray before we eat.

FORBIDDING MARRIAGE

Now the Holy Spirit tells us clearly that in the last
times some will turn away from the true faith;
they will follow deceptive spirits and teachings
that come from demons. These people are
hypocrites and liars, and their consequences are
dead.
They will say it is wrong to be married...

— 1 TIMOTHY 4:1-3

We haven't seen it yet, at the time of this writing, but you will see it according to the Bible. There will not simply be a redefinition of marriage; marriage between a man and a woman will be viewed as wrong and harmful. That's why the Devil hates the Bible; you can actually preach against him and warn people against what he's going to do before he even does it because you've got the whole playbook in the Bible.

SIGNS IN THE HEAVENS

Do you find it odd that the United States, under the Trump Administration, made another military branch called Space Force? Do you think that's going to lead somewhere? I think it's interesting that they recently declassified all the information on UFO's that the government has seen. The Pentagon has admitted to reports of objects in the sky that don't operate under the normal laws of physics. The Director of National Intelligence, in a report dated June 25, 2021[1], describes the threat posed by unidentified aerial phenomena. The US government is gearing up to share the reality of UFOs with the public; this is out in the mainstream media.

The focus on spacecraft and aliens is the preparation of the Devil to explain away the Rapture. What do you think they're going to say when 800 million people disappear off the face of the earth? "Oh my God, we missed the Rapture." No. It'll lead right to everybody wanting to get a chip in their hands so they can be tracked and "kept safe" from abduction. Just look at what people are willing to do for a virus that had a 99.7% survival rate; what do you think people are going to be willing to do when this stuff hits the fan?

UNDERMINING THE AUTHENTICITY OF CHRISTIANITY

I expect something like this will happen: the Catholic Church will say, "We have always had the body of Jesus. He never rose from the dead. We can scientifically confirm that this is his body and comes from that time period. We've always known he never rose from the dead. That's why we have the

Shroud of Turin. We've known exactly where it's at, and we feel it's time to let people know; we have all the evidence."

I believe some woke movements will make believing in God's Word look foolish. The Bible says not to believe anyone who contradicts the Word of God. Between aliens and the Catholic Church working to undermine Christianity, there will be an attempt to make you feel like you're a relic from the 1600s if you believe Jesus Christ rose from the dead.

According to Matthew 24:13, those who endure to the end shall be saved. Paul said that even if an angel appeared and preached a contrary gospel, that angel would be cursed (Galatians 1:8).

I don't care if a UFO landed in front of my property right now, and a spaceman got out, did nine miracles, and told me he's the new Messiah. He can kiss off and go back to Hell where he came from. The world will receive a false Messiah, and courts will threaten those who don't go along with the program with jail.

CLIMATE EMERGENCY

In the natural, declaring a climate emergency is another way to steal from people; the end game is to pass a global carbon tax payable to the United Nations. But spiritually, the climate emergency serves to distract people. Instead of seeing famines, earthquakes, floods, and tsunamis and saying, "Oh my gosh! Just like the Bible said, this is another sign that Jesus is coming soon," people will focus on saving and preserving the Earth.

When you see people very concerned about saving the earth, it's a good indication that they're not saved and don't know the Lord. They're so concerned about this planet because it's the only one they will ever have. 2 Peter 3:13 says that we are looking forward to a new Heaven and a new earth. This earth will be destroyed by fire. There's nothing you can do about that. Noah would have wasted his time building walls to keep the flood out. You don't build walls; you build an ark. Forget about taking action to reduce climate change; you couldn't even pray it off. You cannot pray off a prophetic agenda; if God said something's going to happen, it's going to happen. Prepare yourself for it.

Declaring a climate emergency and passing a global carbon tax doesn't even make sense in the natural. They're going to ask America, France, Germany, and other nations to become carbon neutral. Then India and China will refuse to sign on; they are by far the largest polluting countries on Earth. Even if China and India agreed, the proponents of the carbon tax say there would be an extremely slight change over 100 years, not anytime soon. People have said we have about 12 years left before Earth is destroyed if we don't take severe action on this climate emergency, and even the experts that are for the tax say you won't see any effect for at least 100 years, best case scenario. So if there are only 12 years left, you're in deep trouble anyway. Obviously, Satan can't allow people to just view these things and come to their own conclusion, so they're steering people ahead of time. When seeing these strange things happen all over the planet, instead of saying, "Wow. Jesus is coming soon," people are going to say, "We must save the planet." This group of people will include some preachers as well.

Just as you are seeing ministers promote masks and vaccines, you won't see them preaching that Jesus is coming soon and that you must repent and prepare. Instead, you'll hear them echo the same platitudes as CNN and the World Health Organization about responsibility. Watch for when they switch to the full narrative of climate emergency. Just like they shut down their churches for COVID, just as they paused for a 4 week discussion of Black Lives Matter, ignorant preachers will be doing four-week series on taking care of the earth. They're too stupid to see it. One of the greatest blessings of Bible prophecy is that it makes you un-stupid.

The message of the Bible isn't about saving the planet; it's about saving the people on the planet because the planet will be destroyed. A major difference between Christianity and pagan religions is pagan religions teach you to care for the earth while the Bible teaches you that the earth is here to care for you. I'm not here to help cows; cows are here to help me. God created this earth for man; God did not create man to help His number one priority, the earth. God's going to burn the earth up with unquenchable fire; God cares about me way more than animals. Did Jesus teach that or not? *"Not one Sparrow falls from the sky without your father knowing it, and how much more valuable are you to God than sparrows?"* We're not equal. Me and birds aren't equal, me and dogs aren't equal, me and cows aren't equal, me and turtles aren't equal. If a family of turtles has to die so that I can enjoy a plastic straw, that's their problem. I'm not here to help them. Anytime you hear people obsessed with saving the earth, they're not speaking by the Spirit of God. God's obsessed with saving the people of the earth.

A GREAT DECEPTION

> Yet what we suffer now is nothing compared to the
> glory he will reveal to us later. For all creation is
> waiting eagerly for that future day when God
> will reveal who his children really are. Against
> its will, all creation was subjected to God's
> curse. But with eager hope, the creation looks
> forward to the day when it will join God's chil-
> dren in glorious freedom from death and decay.
> For we know that all creation has been groaning
> as in the pains of childbirth right up to the
> present time.
>
> — ROMANS 8:18-22

This Scripture brings a fascinating concept; there's actually a reaction of the earth against sin. As sin and wickedness increase in the last days, it brings about the increase of what we see happening on the earth. Paul wrote that all creation is groaning against the curse of sin. The earth didn't sin against God, but it was subjected to the curse of the human beings living on it. In fact, where I'm living, one week will be 30 degrees and snowing, and the next week will be 81 degrees and sunny. That's called climate change. But for people who can't predict the weather for the same night, thinking they can predict the weather 100 years from now is insane. This is a climate emergency to mask the clear signs of Christ's return, a great deception.

DON'T BE DULLED BY CAROUSING

> "People will be terrified at what they see coming upon the earth, for the powers in the heavens will be shaken. Then everyone will see the Son of Man coming on a cloud with power and great glory. So when all these things begin to happen, stand and look up, for your salvation is near!"
>
> — LUKE 21:26-28

> "Watch out! Don't let your hearts be dulled by carousing and drunkenness…"
>
> — LUKE 21:34

The Bible tells you two of the ingredients to dull your spirit: carousing and drunkenness. Carousing is the activity of enjoying oneself with others in a noisy, lively way. This word, which nobody uses anymore, basically describes young people's lives today; they just go out, party, talk, fill their lives with noise, and live meaningless lives. The Bible says your spirit is dulled when you live like that. Don't let that day catch you unaware. When people backslide, they don't go to bed one night on fire for God and wake up the next morning backslidden.

What you're doing right now is the opposite of carousing and drunkenness; you're studying the Word, knowing how it brings peace and makes you clear-headed and alert. You can spot an antichrist politician; you can't be deceived. The Bible makes you difficult to deceive, where you're not stupid, where you won't blindly believe everything you're told.

AS IT WAS IN THE DAYS OF LOT

> One day the Pharisees asked Jesus, "When will the
> kingdom of God come?"
> Jesus replied, "The Kingdom of God can't be
> detected by visible signs. You won't be able to
> say, 'Here it is!' or 'It's over there!' For the
> Kingdom of God is already among you."
> Then he said to his disciples, "The time is coming
> when you will long to see the day when the Son
> of Man returns, but you won't see it. People will
> tell you, "Look, there is the Son of Man,' or
> 'Here he is,' but don't go out and follow them.
> For as the lightning flashes and lights up the sky
> from one end of the other, so it will be on the day
> when the Son of Man comes. But first the Son of
> Man must suffer terribly and be rejected by this
> generation.
> "When the Son of Man returns, it will be like it was
> in Noah's day. In those days, people enjoyed
> banquets and parties and weddings right up to
> the time Noah entered his boat and the flood
> came and destroyed them all.
> "And the world will be as it was in the days of Lot."
>
> — LUKE 17:20-28

Lot lived in Sodom and Gomorrah. Genesis 19 says these cities were obsessed with homosexuality, not cities that just had gay people in them. Two angels visited Lot, and the men of the city gathered and beat on the door, shouting, "Send those men out here so that we can all have sex with them." Lot came to the door and said, "Don't do such a wicked thing, let me give you my daughters instead." The men replied, "Do you think you can tell us what to do? We'll kill you if you don't send those men out so we can have sex with them." As it was in the days of Lot, so it will be in the days when the Son of Man returns.

I'm not even an old man, and we didn't have that when I was young. If someone was gay, they kept it to themselves. It was not celebrated, even by sinners. Now we have public schools wanting to teach homosexuality to 4-year-olds in school; Jesus said that's a fulfillment of Bible prophecy.

This is why I said last year that COVID-19 would not cause a 40% unemployment rate, and all the nations would not be shut down. Because there will not be a pre-apocalypse before the apocalypse. It's imperative to know there will not be some kind of massive destruction of the earth, then some years later, the Rapture happens, and the Antichrist takes over. Jesus said that before we leave the earth, people will go about their daily business, eating and drinking, buying and selling, farming and building. It will be business-as-usual right up until the day when the Son of Man returns. Therefore, if you're not looking at things through the lens of Bible prophecy, you won't even know anything's going on. Just like millions of people now have no idea that anything is out of the ordinary; they just wake up, go to work, come home, eat and go back to sleep. It wasn't until the morning that Lot left Sodom, then fire and burning sulfur rained down from Heaven and destroyed all in the city.

> On that day a person out on the deck of a roof must
> not go down into the house to pack. A person out
> in the field must not return home.

> — LUKE 17:31

Remember what happened to Lot's wife. If you cling to your life, you will lose it. But if you let your life go, you will save it.

> That night two people will be asleep in one bed; one
> will be taken, the other left. Two women will be
> grinding flour together at the mill; one will be
> taken, the other left."

"Where will this happen, Lord?" the disciples asked.
Jesus replied, "Just as the gathering of vultures
    shows there is a carcass nearby, so these signs
    indicate that the end is near."

— LUKE 17:34-35,37

Any time there's an increase in demonic power, there's an increase in angelic power to help those called to salvation. Get in the flow of the Holy Ghost. Stay with God and His Word. If they want to treat you like you're some leftover from the 1800s, buy a pair of overalls and a straw hat and eat a steak. If the world doesn't like you, you're on the right track. If the world thinks you're doing great, you're probably going to Hell. Wear it as a badge of honor when the world hates you. Your boldness will inspire other people to do the same.

Everything you have read thus far is not just information to understand; this present age is ending. There really is a Heaven, there really is a Hell, and every person will spend their eternity in one of those two places. That decision is not made by God; that decision is made by you. Choose Christ. Choose life. Choose the blessing.

ELEVEN THINGS YOU MUST DO KNOWING CHRIST IS COMING

THE PURPOSE OF PROPHECY

Bible prophecy can cause you to live paralyzed by fear if you're not careful. If you live in fear, it shows that you didn't get the spirit of the Word of God that was behind the prophecy. The Bible says end-time prophecy brings comfort and encouragement to a Christian. It should only unsettle you if you don't know the Lord.

> This is my second letter to you, dear friends, and in
> both of them I have tried to stimulate your
> wholesome thinking and refresh your memory. I
> want you to remember what the holy prophets
> said long ago and what our Lord and Savior
> commanded through your apostles.
> Most importantly, I want to remind you that in the
> last days scoffers will come, mocking the truth
> and following their own desires. They will say,
> "What happened to the promise that Jesus is
> coming again? From before the times of our

ancestors, everything has remained the same
since the world was first created."

They deliberately forget that God made the heavens
long ago by the word of his command, and he
brought the earth out from the water and
surrounded it with water. Then he used the water
to destroy the ancient world with a mighty flood.
And by the same word, the present heavens and
earth have been stored up for fire. They are being
kept for the day of judgment, when ungodly
people will be destroyed.

But you must not forget this one thing, dear friends:
A day is like a thousand years to the Lord, and a
thousand years is like a day. The Lord isn't really
being slow about his promise, as some people
think. No, he is being patient for your sake. He
does not want anyone to be destroyed, but wants
everyone to repent. But the day of the Lord will
come as unexpectedly as a thief. Then the
heavens will pass away with a terrible noise, and
the very elements themselves will disappear in
fire, and the earth and everything on it will be
found to deserve judgment.

Since everything around us is going to be destroyed
like this, what holy and godly lives you should
live, looking forward to the day of God and
hurrying it along. On that day, he will set the
heavens on fire, and the elements will melt away
in the flames. But we are looking forward to the
new heavens and new earth he has promised, a
world filled with God's righteousness.

And so, dear friends, while you are waiting for these
things to happen, make every effort to be found
living peaceful lives that are pure and blameless
in his sight.

> And remember, our Lord's patience gives people
> time to be saved…
>
> — 2 PETER 3:1-15

The purpose of Bible prophecy is to motivate you to spread the Gospel, not to paralyze you with fright. The Lord is waiting so that people have time to be saved.

Bible prophecy enables you to live on this earth knowing the end game and to make good life decisions.

ELEVEN THINGS YOU MUST DO

Based on Bible prophecy, let's review eleven things you must do, knowing Christ is coming soon.

Number One: Adopt a Passover Mentality

> Then those who feared the Lord spoke with each
> other, and the Lord listened to what they said. In
> his presence, a scroll of remembrance was
> written to record the names of those who feared
> him and always thought about the honor of his
> name.
> "They will be my people," says the Lord of Heaven's Armies. "On the day when I act in judgment, they will be my own special treasure. I
> will spare them as a father spares an obedient
> child. Then you will again see the difference
> between the righteous and the wicked, between
> those who serve God and those who do not."
>
> — MALACHI 3:16-18

> The Lord of Heaven's Armies says, "The day of
> judgment is coming, burning like a furnace. On
> that day, the arrogant and the wicked will be
> burned up like straw. They will be consumed —
> root, branches, and all.
> "But for you who fear my name, the Sun of Right-
> eousness will rise with healing in his wings. And
> you will go free, leaping with joy like calves let
> out to pasture. On the day when I act, you will
> tread upon the wicked as if they were dust under
> your feet."
>
> — MALACHI 4:1-3

You won't be duped into fearfulness if you properly understand Bible prophecy. When COVID-19 hit last year, did you notice some people were convinced that it was "the end"? But, it's not time for that until after the Rapture.

You must have a Passover mentality.

There will be a visible difference between the righteous and the wicked, between those who serve God and those who do not. I live in this world, but what affects the people of this world is not permitted to affect me.

In Psalm 91, God said, "I'll order my angels to protect you wherever you go. Though 1,000 fall at your one side and 10,000 are falling all around you, these evils will not touch you."

He said, "I give you authority over all the power of the Devil, and nothing will harm you. You will trample on serpents and scorpions and subdue them under your feet."

According to Malachi 4:2, on the day of judgment, the Sun of Righteousness will rise with healing in his wings.

> For the LORD will pass through the land to strike
> down the Egyptians. But when he sees the blood
> on the top and sides of the doorframe, the LORD
> will pass over your home. He will not permit his
> death angel to enter your house and strike you
> down.
>
> — EXODUS 12:23

We need a Passover mentality; what touches this world is not permitted to touch us.

Number Two: Live to Occupy

An old saying amongst Pentecostals is to live like Jesus is coming today, but plan like Jesus is never coming.

According to Enoch Adobe, following a revival that ballooned the Redeemed Christian Church of God in Nigeria, the newly saved people said, "Well, let's just sit and sing and wait for Jesus to come." But that's not what the Bible teaches you to do. A righteous man leaves an inheritance to his children's children. He had to sit people down and tell them, "You need to go to school. You need to get a job. You need to live."

You need to advance. If the purpose of Bible prophecy were to get people to say, "Who cares about this world anyway; I'm getting out of here," then I wouldn't be preaching the Gospel and building the Kingdom of God.

God never changes. The same God who told you to be fruitful and multiply in Genesis still expects fruitfulness and multiplication, even more so in the last days as the time runs short.

> For the Son of man is come to seek and to save that
> which was lost.
> And as they heard these things, he added and spake a
> parable, because he was nigh to Jerusalem, and

> because they thought that the kingdom of God
> should immediately appear.
> He said therefore, A certain nobleman went into a far
> country to receive for himself a kingdom. and to
> return.
> And he called his ten servants, and delivered them
> ten pounds, and said unto them, Occupy till I
> come.
>
> — LUKE 19:10-13 (KJV)

Jesus said, "Occupy till I come." He did not say to dig a hole and wait for Him to come. In the Dake Reference Bible, the author's note says, "Engage in business until I come."

Live like He's coming today; plan like He's never coming.

Number Three: Be Positive and Confident

Knowing Jesus is coming soon, you must refuse to adopt a defeatist worldview. A defeatist worldview sounds like, "The Bible said things are getting worse, and here we are. Can you believe all the stuff that's going on out there? Transgender education and Biden's in now, he's going to cut the oil supply off, and…" Refuse to adopt that worldview. There is no slow ceding of the power of the Church to the Devil. We're in charge until we're gone. So, act like it. Joe Biden doesn't dictate my future. The World Health Organization doesn't dictate my future. Even if the United Nations made it their goal to stop me, nothing I'm doing would even slow down. No one has the power to stop me because I'm hooked up with God. Whatever can't stop Christ can't stop in you. The evil in this world will never be greater than the Holy Ghost who lives in you. The Devil is under my feet today. He'll be under my feet tomorrow. He'll be under my feet when I go to Heaven. He's not getting more powerful in the last days; he's the same defeated schmuck that he was in 1810.

When Donald Trump lost the election, you would have thought Jesus died. I prospered when Obama was in office. I prospered when Trump was in office. I'm prospering with Biden in office. I'll prosper when whoever else will be in office. I'm in a different kingdom. Your mind cannot be dwelling on what your enemy is doing. If three of every five social media posts you make are about what the Devil, the Illuminati, or globalist powers are doing, you've lost it. You're not full of the Holy Ghost, you do not pray in tongues, and you're not in the anointing. I've never—not one time—spent time with God praying in tongues and came out of it saying, "Man, we're really in trouble."

You will not have a defeatist worldview when you're confident in God.

Number Four: Build a Strong Marriage

> ...As for me and my house, we will serve the Lord.
>
> — JOSHUA 24:15 (KJV)

Invest in your spouse and control your home. You can't control what goes on outside your house, but you can control what goes on inside your house. Many people get preoccupied with what the government's doing. It becomes like mental marijuana that they use to escape from the fact that their marriage is a mess, they're terrible at raising their kids, they don't make any money, and their life is an overall wreck. So they focus on what the Devil is doing as an escape, just like one would with a video game.

If you're a wife, invest in your husband. Make Jesus number 1 and your husband 1A. Don't think about how he treats you; think about how you treat him. I know that's not popular to say nowadays, but nothing I say is, so I might as well stay consistent. I'm sure many women will disagree with me, but it works.

If you're a husband, Jesus is your number 1; your wife is 1A. Treat her like gold. Do you even know your wife's favorite restaurant? For example, when my wife mentioned she wanted to start biking, I went ahead and got a bike assembled for her. Why? Because I treat her like I would treat Jesus. If Jesus mentioned he'd like a bike, there'd be a bike even if I had to sell one of my kidneys. You have a physical representation of Jesus—your wife—

who you need to treat like you would treat God. If you want to dump out your alabaster box on Jesus, dump one out on your spouse.

Everything the Devil wants to do starts with breaking up the family, so make yours extra strong. The greatest way you can rebel against what the Devil wants to do in the government is to build a strong marriage with strong, faith-filled children.

Number Five: Invest in Your Children

In the same vein, invest in your children. The Bible says to train your children in the fear and admonition of the Lord; raise up a child in the way they should go, and when they grow old, they will not depart from it. Keep an eye on your children. This is how you fight the antichrist spirit trying to penetrate the world.

You don't start addressing the fact that your 15-year-old doesn't want to go to church anymore when they're 15; it actually started when they were 8, and you had them on their knees in the pew playing on an iPad. It started when the church leaders said, "everyone stand up for praise and worship," and you allowed your kid to stay playing on their iPad. Your home is not a democracy; your home has a leader. God didn't call Abraham, Sarah, and Isaac together and say, "If you guys are all cool with it, I'd like y'all to go up and sacrifice Isaac on top of the mountain. You can discuss it amongst yourselves." Instead, God directed Abraham, and Abraham enforced it.

Train them. Tell your child to stand up and lift their hands. It doesn't matter if they don't really want to. They don't really want to brush their teeth or wipe their rear ends either, but you make them. You train them and teach them *all* things in life, especially spiritual things.

As soon as you see them disconnect from God in the slightest, deal with it. Don't wait until it's a huge problem. Do you have them in a crap church with no anointing? Have you allowed your child to grow up in a church that, although they are 13-years-old, they have still never been baptized in the Holy Ghost, speaking in tongues? What are you doing? Stop focusing on things you can't control and focus on things God gave you authority over. Training your kids matters.

"Should I hide my plan from Abraham?" the Lord
asked. "For Abraham will certainly become a
great and mighty nation, and all the nations of
the earth will be blessed through him. I have
singled him out..."

— GENESIS 18:17-19

God singled Abraham out because He knew Abraham would do as directed
and train his family. You don't need to be a tyrant to train your children. If
you're doing it right, you won't have to force your children to attend
church. My dad never had to say, "No, you're not allowed to go to your
hockey game, it's on a church night." I never asked because I knew; I'm a
full-time Christian and a part-time everything else. For example, if you say
your boss tells you that you have to work on Sunday, I don't think you
know what being a Christian is. My life is not in the hands of my boss. My
life is in my hands, and I choose to serve the Lord; anyone who tries to get
in the way of that will be sorry they did.

God set Abraham apart for a blessing because Abraham put God first.
Abraham was a God-man. God first. God only. God in the morning. God in
the afternoon. God at night. You need to model that for your children. You
cannot have your children in the world all week and still stay connected to
God. You have received the spirit of the Church, not the spirit of the world.
If you have them in public school 40 hours a week, then add in dance
team, travel baseball, cheer, etc., then you take them to church twice a
month, they'll go to Hell. You cannot have them in the world more than
they're in Christ and hope things will somehow work out. No, they'll go to
Hell. If you're raising them in the world, then doing church as a side thing,
they're going to be world-people, not church-people. I know I sound like a
90-year-old man, but I don't care. Don't send your kids to places where
they'll get a love for the things of the world. Parents, you need to know
this: you can command your children to serve the Lord. Command your
house so that people know they will serve the Lord if they live there; that's
not barking orders that they're to be a Christian. It would have been

impossible for someone to grow up and not serve the Lord with my parents.

If you treat your child right, they don't want to displease you because they love you. My daughter Camila is devastated if she feels we don't approve of something she did. Keep their spirits tender and pray with them at night before you send them to bed. Don't have a home where everybody's in their own corner of the house. Invest in your children.

Number Six: Tie Your Life to Kingdom Advancement

> ...Seek ye first the kingdom of God, and his right-
> eousness; and when you do, all these things shall
> be added unto you.
>
> — MATTHEW 6:33 (KJV)

Tie your life to advancing God's kingdom. If I asked your pastor about you, does he even know who you are? Or do you just show up, sit two-thirds of the way back, and leave immediately when the meeting is over? What are you doing every week that's tied to advancing God's kingdom? Going to church is not serving God; going to church is God serving you. Other people have worked, studied, and prepared to minister to you, but what of your life is tied to advancing God's kingdom?

> Seek the Kingdom of God above all else, and live
> righteously, and he will give you everything you
> need.
>
> — MATTHEW 6:33

Matthew 6:33 is the golden scripture of the New Testament. As I advance God's kingdom, God will provide for me everything other people die trying to get. A man that's tied in with the advancement of God's kingdom can't sink. If you tie yourself to God's kingdom, you cannot be sunk, and your finances cannot be sunk. King David's secret was setting his affection on the house of the Lord; he cared about God's kingdom.

I'm invested in a stock that had its earnings report live-streamed a while ago. They opened it up for questions, but people like me that owned a few shares were not the people who called in; the people who were heavily invested called in, and the CEO knew them. That's what it's like to be tied in. How heavily invested in God's kingdom are you?

Do you own a business? Be a kingdom man or woman and have your business tied to advancing the kingdom, then watch how God blesses it.

Recently, we did a 1-hour worldwide television special. We had over 2,700 people call in for prayer. 91 people volunteered to answer phones; they took time out of their busy lives to pray with people. The volunteers wrote me, one after another, saying things like, "That was the most rewarding thing I've ever done. I'm still teary-eyed from being able to pray with them." Yet, you think you're giving something up for the kingdom just by showing up at church.

> If you try to hang on to your life, you will lose it.
> But if you give up your life for my sake and for
> the sake of the Good News, you will save it.

> — MARK 8:35

Number Seven: Connect Your Money to Kingdom Advancement

Tie your money into advancing God's kingdom. The tithes and the offering shield you from the economic horrors that will come on the earth. God said, "I will rebuke the devourer for your sake."

Why is this important for the last days? Because there's going to be a devourer that comes after people's money, and God said He will protect you. There's a shield around the provision of God's children, and the windows of Heaven open. The United Nations doesn't control the windows of Heaven. The World Economic Forum doesn't control the windows of

Heaven; God does. Many people can testify to this because they tied their money to God's kingdom in 2020; while everyone else complained about finances, they kept their mouths shut. This is not a book of good ideas; this is a book of laws. Laws that don't fail.

> It is like a person building a house who digs deep
> and lays the foundation on solid rock. When the
> floodwaters rise and break against that house, it
> stands firm because it is well built.
>
> — LUKE 6:48

> "Bring all the tithes into the storehouse so there will
> be enough food in my Temple. If you do," says
> the Lord of Heaven's Armies, "I will open the
> windows of heaven for you. I will pour out a
> blessing so great you won't have enough room to
> take it in!"
>
> — MALACHI 3:10

Number Eight: Be a Soul-Winner

Knowing that Christ is coming soon, you must win souls. The Lord is waiting so people have time to be saved. In the same way, you give with ferocity, go after lost souls with ferocity. Go after the lost; stand in front of crowds who are not Christian and get them saved. The laborer is paid good wages.

The Bible says how beautiful are the feet of them that preach the good news and the Gospel of Jesus Christ! The highest thing anyone can ever do is give himself to win lost souls for God. That's why Paul said, *my God shall supply all your needs, according to his riches*, because he was addressing those who gave to further the Gospel.

If you support evangelism, if you, yourself, evangelize and you give yourself to saving the lost, doing so will bring greater blessing on your life than any other thing you could ever do because that's the heart of Jesus.

Number Nine: Enjoy Worldly Reproach

Learn to enjoy the reproach of the world. Learn to enjoy the fact that as they hated Christ, they will hate you too. I'm not talking about going out of your way to be a jerk. Churches didn't shut down because they were afraid of a virus; churches shut down because they were afraid of mean comments on Facebook. The modern Western Christian cannot deal with shame and reproach from the world; they think it's a mark of honor for the world to like you. As a follower of Christ, it's actually an honor to bear the shame and reproach from the world. Paul said in Galatians 6:17, "*I bear on my body the scars that show I belong to Jesus.*" He had actual physical wounds that people gave him, proving he was anointed.

In Acts chapter 7, when Stephen was going to preach, it doesn't say he heard of angry people who would pick up rocks to throw at him, so he just decided now probably isn't the best time. No, it says he preached. The crowd ground their teeth and started launching stones at him, then Jesus stood up and received Stephen into Heaven.

Number Ten: Don't Be Lulled to Sleep

Don't be lulled to sleep by this world. Luke 21:34 says to watch out.

> "Watch out! Don't let your hearts be dulled by
> carousing and drunkenness, and by the worries
> of this life. Don't let that day catch you unaware,
> like a trap. For that day will come upon everyone
> living on the earth. Keep alert at all times. And
> pray that you might be strong enough to escape
> these coming horrors and stand before the Son of
> Man."
>
> — LUKE 21:34-36

The worries of this life have the same effect of lulling you to sleep spiritu-ally or making your spirit cold and indifferent, just as drugs, alcohol, and partying do. There might be more people who don't go to church anymore and have a lukewarm relationship with God, not because they fell into drugs, but due to the worries of this life. Why? Because they've built their life the way they teach you to in America; they don't own anything, they don't buy what they can afford, they buy what they can afford the payments on with the help of credit cards. They've organized their life improperly and have become a slave to the world. Don't let your fire go out because of the cares of this world or the desire for nice things. Keep an eye on your spirit, don't allow it to become lazy, cold, and indifferent. Every night before you go to sleep, you've either been pulled closer to God during that day, or you've fallen back. There is no neutral.

> Don't you realize that in a race everyone runs, but
> only one person gets the prize? So run to win!
> All athletes are disciplined in their training. They
> do it to win a prize that will fade away, but we
> do it for an eternal prize. So I run with purpose
> in every step. I am not just shadowboxing. I

discipline my body like an athlete, training it to
do what it should. Otherwise, I fear that after
preaching to others I myself might be
disqualified.

— 1 CORINTHIANS 9:24-27

Number Eleven: Lose Your Fascination with Sin

Since everything around us is going to be destroyed,
what holy and godly lives you should live,
looking forward to the day of God and hurrying
it along.

— 2 PETER 3:11-12

Don't be lulled into sin, live holy. For example, men, you can't take women you're not married to out to eat; that's how affairs start. Keep a watch on yourself for the beginnings of being lulled into sin. Where are you spending time? Who are you spending time with? Who are you listening to? What new people have you allowed into your life that pull you away from God? Adam and Eve lost the garden; they listened to the serpent, who planted doubt about God's words. Are the new people in your life sent from God to strengthen you, or are they sent from the Devil to lull you into sin?

Don't fall in love with God's forgiveness, like they teach you in Western church; "No matter what we do, God forgives." If you go through life with that motto, you'll probably end up in Hell.

Well then, since God's grace has set us free from the
law, does that mean we can go on sinning? Of
course not!

— ROMANS 6:15

When I'm preaching to a crowd of sinners, I'll tell them that God will forgive whatever they've done. But my life's motto is not: "Well, whatever I do today, God will forgive me." If you start adopting these Western mottos, you will go to Hell. In John 8, Jesus told the woman, *"Neither do I condemn you; go and sin no more."* In John 5, He said, *"You have been made well. Sin no more, lest a worse thing come upon you.."* He didn't say "sin less"; He said stop. Knock sin out of your lane and knock anyone out of your life who teaches you to accept sin. Treat any pastor, Bible teacher, or preacher who makes soft comments towards sin like cancer.

Holy, holy, holy is the Lord God almighty. Who can appear before the Lord on His mountain? Only those with pure hands and a clean heart. Holiness is the master key. This world is getting more wicked by the hour, but don't join them.

> Oh, the joys of those who do not follow the advice
> of the wicked, or stand around with sinners or
> join in with mockers.
>
> — PSALM 1:1

According to the Bible, where I *stand* matters, where I *sit* matters, and where I *go* matters. There are places I don't belong. If you go through all of my Instagram posts, you won't see me at some concert. I'm not one of them; I don't belong there. They're all welcome to come hear me preach, I want them to get saved, but I'm not going there. Cardi B is not my psalmist. Taylor Swift is not my worship leader. I'm a God man. Yet, you would be hard-pressed to have more fun in life than I have. This isn't about divorcing yourself from fun; it is about divorcing yourself from sin.

Jesse Duplantis said, "Money will make you comfortable while you're miserable." People in the world aren't having fun moving in and out of marriages, fighting in their homes, or dulling their pain with substance abuse. My father would say, "Sin will cost you more than you mean to pay. Sin will keep you longer than you want to stay. Sin will take you where you don't want to go." Lose the fascination with sin; it's an illusion that ends in death. The pleasure phase of sin wears off very quickly.

Get out of a church where they preach from the pulpit, "We all have weaknesses." Realize that there are places you don't belong as a child of God.

> Who may climb the mountain of the LORD?
> Who may stand in his holy place?
> Only those whose hands and hearts are pure, who do
> not worship idols and never tell lies.
>
> — PSALM 24:3-4

You can't clean your own hands, and you can't purify your own heart; you need Jesus. If you've never given your life to Jesus Christ, do that right now. Get your life squared away with God.

AFTERWORD

What are you willing to die for? It's time to decide.

We're coming to a predicted and decided ending. But we're not placed here to be dominated by the Antichrist and simply hang on until Jesus comes. We are here to restrain evil until the appointed ending.

But if you cower and hide, what good are you? You'll get washed downstream if you get into the river of compromise. You'll end up doing whatever it takes to be a state-accepted church. Defy the Devil.

When the day comes that the Devil presses you, stand and fight. The Devil wants you to give up even though he has no power to stop a Christian who won't lie down. Demon-possessed people can't override what God said in the Bible; there's no double standard.

Christ is not coming back for a weak, defeated, beat-up Church. He's coming back for a glorious Church without spot or wrinkle. I want you to make up your mind that you will be a part of that Church today.

If you have never accepted Jesus Christ as your Savior, you can take care of that right now, right where you are. There is no decision you can make that's more impactful than this. Pray this prayer aloud and receive God's forgiveness and salvation:

> Heavenly Father, I believe that you raised Jesus from the dead. I give you my life today and confess that Jesus is my Lord and Savior. I turn my back on sin and receive your forgiveness. I want to live for you. In Jesus' name, amen.

If you prayed that prayer, tell me about your decision, so we can send you some materials to help you get started in your new life. Go to this link: revivaltoday.com/just-got-saved.

The Revival Today Staff is available to pray with you. Call 412-787-2578 to speak and pray with a real, living person who cares about you.

Congratulations on making the most important decision of your life, and welcome to the family of God!

NOTES

CHAPTER 1

1. *Boko Haram: Unease Over Murder Of Redeemed Christian Pastor In Borno | Sahara Reporters.* (n.d.). Saharareporters.com. Retrieved November 29, 2022, from https://saharareporters.com/2014/07/19/boko-haram-unease-over-murder-redeemed-christian-pastor-borno

CHAPTER 4

1. *Why do young Americans love leftism? | Be sure to subscribe at PragerU.com! | By Dennis Prager | Facebook.* (n.d.). Www.facebook.com. Retrieved November 28, 2022, from https://fb.watch/h4IDF5OfTX/

2. Caryle Murphy. (2015, December 18). *Most U.S. Christian groups grow more accepting of homosexuality.* Pew Research Center; Pew Research Center. https://www.pewresearch.org/fact-tank/2015/12/18/most-u-s-christian-groups-grow-more-accepting-of-homosexuality/

3. (2019, September 23). *Are George Soros' "Rented Evangelicals" Trying to Rewrite the Bible?* [Review of *Are George Soros' "Rented Evangelicals" Trying to Rewrite the Bible?*]. Pulpitandpen.org. https://pulpitandpen.org/2019/09/23/are-george-soros-rented-evangelicals-trying-to-rewrite-the-bible/

4. Boorstein, M. (2018, January 18). Trump's evangelical advisers, with Pelosi, push for 'dreamers.' *Washington Post.* https://www.washingtonpost.com/news/acts-of-faith/wp/2018/01/18/evangelical-advisers-to-president-trump-meet-with-pelosi-to-push-for-solution-for-dreamers/

CHAPTER 5

1. Courtois, S., & Kramer, M. (1999). *The black book of communism : crimes, terror, repression.* Harvard University Press.

CHAPTER 7

1. Iraq Suffers as the Euphrates River Dwindles. (2009, July 14). *The New York Times.* https://www.nytimes.com/2009/07/14/world/middleeast/14euphrates.html

CHAPTER 9

1. *Preliminary Assessment: Unidentified Aerial Phenomena.* (2021). https://www.dni.gov/files/ODNI/documents/assessments/Prelimary-Assessment-UAP-20210625.pdf

"My generation shall be saved."

— JONATHAN SHUTTLESWORTH

EVANGELIST AND PASTOR
JONATHAN SHUTTLESWORTH

Evangelist and Pastor, Jonathan Shuttlesworth, is the founder of Revival Today and Pastor of Revival Today Church, ministries dedicated to reaching lost and hurting people with The Gospel of Jesus Christ.

In fulfilling his calling, Jonathan Shuttlesworth has conducted meetings and open-air crusades throughout North America, India, the Caribbean, and Central and South Africa.

Revival Today Church was launched in 2022 as a soul-winning, Holy Spirit honoring church that is unapologetic about believing the Bible to bless families and nations.

Each day thousands of lives are impacted globally through Revival Today Broadcasting and Revival Today Church, located in Pittsburgh, Pennsylvania.

While methods may change, Revival Today's heartbeat remains for the lost, providing biblical teaching on faith, healing, prosperity, freedom from sin, and living a victorious life.

If you need help or want to partner with Revival Today to see this generation and nation transformed through The Gospel, follow these links.

CONTACT REVIVAL TODAY

www.RevivalToday.com
www.RevivalTodayChurch.com
412-440-1412

facebook.com/revivaltoday
twitter.com/jdshuttlesworth
instagram.com/jdshuttlesworth
youtube.com/RevivalToday07